THE ASIAN
Slow Cooker

THE ASIAN

Slow Cooker

EXOTIC FAVORITES FOR YOUR CROCKPOT

KELLY KWOK FOUNDER OF LIFE MADE SWEETER

PAGE STREET
PUBLISHING CO.

PAGE STREET
PUBLISHING CO.

First published in 2016 by

Page Street Publishing Co.

27 Congress Street, Suite 105

Salem, MA 01970

www.pagestreetpublishing.com

Distributed by Macmillan; sales in Canada by The Canadian Manda Group; distribution in Canada by The Jaguar Book Group.

19   18   17   16   1   2   3   4   5

ISBN-13: 978-1-62414-290-1

ISBN-10: 1-62414-290-7

Library of Congress Control Number: 2016944701

Cover and book design by Page Street Publishing Co.

Photography by Kelly Kwok

Printed and bound in The United States

Page Street is proud to be a member of 1% for the Planet. Members donate one percent of their sales to one or more of the over 1,500 environmental and sustainability charities across the globe who participate in this program.

TO MY LOVING MOM,
FOR TEACHING ME THE JOYS OF BEING IN THE KITCHEN
FROM THE VERY BEGINNING.
THANK YOU FOR ENCOURAGING ME TO CHASE MY
DREAMS NO MATTER WHAT.

TO MY DEAR FAMILY,
FOR MAKING LIFE SWEETER EVERY DAY.

IN LOVING MEMORY OF MY GUARDIAN ANGELS,
WHO ARE ALWAYS CLOSE TO MY HEART.

Contents

Introduction

We didn't grow up with a slow cooker in our house. In fact, I don't think my parents even knew what it was.

They were both great cooks and taught the three of us kids how to make freshly prepared meals at an early age. Like most traditional Chinese cooks, there was no measuring—just a pinch of this and a handful of that from their experience and eyeballing. By the time we were in high school, my brothers and I would take turns making dinner and adding our own spins on the meals we made.

It wasn't until my husband and I got married that I started experimenting with the slow cooker we received for Christmas that year. We both worked long hours during the week so I loved the idea of having a hot meal waiting for us when we got home.

At first I was just sticking to the basics and making mostly soups and stews. Then once we had our son, my time in the kitchen had to be quick, which took a lot of fun out of cooking. I started to miss the comforting meals I grew up making as well as our favorite restaurant dishes. Dining out with a baby was challenging at times, so we didn't go out to eat much when he was younger.

This led me to want to learn how to make our favorite restaurant dishes at home. Using my slow cooker meant I could still finish folding the laundry or play with our son while our meal was cooking. As he got older, things got a little bit easier, and I was able to spend more time in the kitchen again.

It was during this time that I started my blog, Life Made Sweeter. It became my creative outlet and I found a new joy for cooking again. My son was a great eater and became my inspiration for many of the recipes I made.

When my daughter was born, my time in the kitchen fixing our meals became much more challenging again. She was (and still is) extremely attached to me, and would cry if my husband, my mom or anyone other than me tried to hold her. So now with two young kids in the kitchen by my feet, I once again turned to my trusty slow cooker to help me get dinner on the table.

The slow cooker was such a lifesaver for me during those busy weeknights. I could quickly prep the ingredients I needed when my youngest was taking her afternoon nap and toss everything into the crock pot. That way, when she woke up, dinner would still be cooking, but I wouldn't have to be stirring anything by the stove when both the kids wanted my attention during their restless hours. It worked out great, because we would all get to eat a hot meal by the time my husband got home from work.

This book covers some of my favorite Asian recipes that can be partially or fully made in the slow cooker, as well as common skillet and one-pot wonders. They include traditional dishes I grew up making, food from my travels through Asia, popular takeout favorites, hidden restaurant gems, modern twists on classics, kid-friendly meals and delectable desserts.

Some of these use shortcuts with only 5 ingredients or less, along with easy set-and-forget meals, making them perfect for busy weeknights. Then there are those that call for traditional from-scratch ingredients along with browning or sautéing things before placing them in the slow cooker.

All of these recipes are meant for anyone who wants to explore new and exciting ways to prepare Asian cuisine at home. I believe making them in the slow cooker helps to take the fear out of cooking with traditional and unfamiliar Asian ingredients, since it does most of the work for you. It minimizes worry about burning food, and can help to enhance flavor development. Plus it saves you time with the ability to plan ahead.

Using the slow cooker to create meals that I grew up on and feel a strong cultural connection with has allowed me to appreciate making meals for my family again.

I discovered that you can cook a lot more than soups and stews in the slow cooker.

Most of all, I hope these recipes inspire YOU to use your slow cooker in ways you never thought possible.

Kelly

Ditch the Takeout

We all have those busy weeknights when all we want to do is forget about making dinner and order our favorite dishes from the local takeout restaurant.

Who can resist slurping up the classic Chicken Lo Mein noodles with a plate of Orange Beef, Teriyaki Chicken and Korean-Style Short Ribs?

You can easily make these popular takeout dishes right in your own kitchen using the slow cooker, while saving some extra money. There is nothing better than coming home to a hot meal that's been simmering away while you are gone. With this collection of crowd-pleasing recipes, you can eat takeout every single night of the week without even having to leave your home!

HELPFUL HINTS

- Most of the dishes in this chapter call for prebrowning the meat for a few minutes on the stove in order to achieve optimal results to mimic the rich flavor and crispy texture of most takeout restaurants. For a simpler version or if low on time, you can easily skip this added step.

- The key to many of these dishes lies in the thick and flavorful sauce. Some slow cookers tend to have lower levels of heating elements (particularly older models) so the sauce may not thicken up properly. If that is the case, simply spoon it out from the slow cooker into a small saucepan and bring to a boil on high heat until it thickens up.

- Remember that coating the inside of the slow cooker with cooking spray prior to adding food helps to prevent sticking.

BEEF & BROCCOLI

This popular takeout dish showed up at our dinner table weekly when I was growing up. It was one of the very first dishes my parents taught me how to make when I learned how to cook. The key to keeping the broccoli crisp is tossing it into the slow cooker right near the end. Combined with the tender strips of beef and rich savory sauce, it's an easy weeknight meal you'll want to make again and again.

YIELD: 4 SERVINGS

½ cup plus 1½ tbsp (78 g) cornstarch, divided

½ tsp salt

¼ tsp black pepper

1 lb (455 g) flank steak, cut across the grain into thin strips

2 tsp (10 ml) cooking oil

1 cup (237 ml) beef broth

½ cup (118 ml) low sodium soy sauce

⅓ cup (65 g) brown sugar

2 tbsp (32 g) oyster sauce

1 tsp sesame oil

3 garlic cloves, minced

1 tsp minced fresh ginger

2 tbsp (30 ml) cold water

2½ cups (210 g) broccoli florets

Cooked rice, for serving

Sesame seeds, for garnish (optional)

In a large zip-top bag, toss together ½ cup (30 g) cornstarch, salt and black pepper. Add the beef to the bag and give it a little shake until well coated.

In a large skillet, heat the cooking oil over medium-high heat. Sear the beef for about 1 to 2 minutes on both sides and add to the slow cooker.

In a medium bowl, whisk together the broth, soy sauce, sugar, oyster sauce, sesame oil, garlic and ginger until dissolved and pour over the beef. Cover with the lid and cook on low for about 3 to 4 hours.

About 30 minutes prior to serving, whisk together the remaining cornstarch with water in a small bowl and stir into the crock pot along with the broccoli, then cover with the lid. Turn the heat to high and allow the sauce to cook and thicken up for about 20 to 30 minutes, until the broccoli is just starting to soften but is tender and crisp.

Serve over rice and garnish with sesame seeds, if desired.

CASHEW CHICKEN

Cashew chicken is one of those amazingly simple recipes that my family has on regular dinner rotation. My son is a big fan of cashews so he always gets excited whenever I tell him we are having this takeout favorite for dinner. The creamy cashews add a delightful crunch and sweet undertone to this savory meal. It's quick, delicious and perfect for those busy weeknights.

YIELD: 4 SERVINGS

2½ tbsp (22 g) cornstarch, divided

1 tsp baking soda

¼ tsp salt

¼ tsp black pepper

1½ lb (683 g) boneless, skinless chicken thighs or breasts, cut into bite-sized cubes

2 tsp (10 ml) cooking oil

⅓ cup (79 ml) low sodium soy sauce

½ cup (118 ml) low sodium chicken broth

1 tbsp (16 g) oyster sauce

2 tbsp (30 ml) Chinese rice wine or dry sherry

3 tbsp (63 g) honey

1 tsp sesame oil

3 cloves garlic, minced

1 tsp fresh ginger, minced

¼ tsp red pepper chili flakes, to taste

2 tbsp (30 ml) cool water

1 green bell pepper, cut into 1" (2.5-cm) chunks

⅔ cups (475 g) unsalted cashews, roasted

Cooked rice, for serving

Sesame seeds, for garnish (optional)

1 green onion, thinly sliced, for garnish (optional)

In a large zip-top bag, toss together 1 tablespoon (10 g) cornstarch, baking soda, salt and black pepper. Next add the chicken to the bag, and give it a little shake until well coated.

In a large skillet, heat the oil over medium-high heat. Cook the chicken, about 2 to 3 minutes on both sides then transfer to the slow cooker.

In a medium bowl, whisk together the soy sauce, broth, oyster sauce, wine, honey, sesame oil, garlic, ginger and chili flakes; then pour over the chicken. Cover and cook on low for about 3 to 4 hours.

About 30 minutes prior to serving, whisk together the remaining cornstarch with water in a small bowl and stir into the slow cooker. Toss in the bell pepper and cashews and stir to combine. Turn the heat to high and allow the sauce to cook and thicken up for about 20 to 30 minutes.

Serve hot over rice. Garnish with sesame seeds and green onions, if desired.

CHICKEN LO MEIN

We are big noodle fans in our house, so you can usually find us slurping up a different bowl for lunch or dinner a few times a week. Chicken Lo Mein is one of our favorites and also one of the most popular recipes on Life Made Sweeter. The tender chicken, crunchy vegetables and long noodles are covered in a flavor-packed sauce that can rival your favorite takeout restaurant.

YIELD: 4 SERVINGS

½ cup (118 ml) low sodium chicken broth

2 tbsp (32 g) oyster sauce

2 tbsp (30 ml) low sodium soy sauce

2 tsp (10 g) hoisin sauce

2 tsp (14 g) honey

½ tsp red pepper chili flakes, optional

2 garlic cloves, minced

½ tbsp (4 g) minced fresh ginger

1 lb (455 g) boneless, skinless chicken thighs or breasts

2 cups (475 g) fresh lo mein noodles or cooked spaghetti noodles

2 cups (475 g) baby bok choy, washed and sliced

1 red bell pepper, seeded, thinly sliced

½ cup (75 g) matchstick carrots

2 tbsp (16 g) cornstarch

3 tbsp (45 ml) cold water

Sesame seeds, for garnish (optional)

Whisk together the broth, oyster sauce, soy sauce, hoisin sauce, honey, chili flakes, garlic and ginger in the slow cooker. Nestle the chicken in the middle and coat with sauce on all sides. Cook for 3 to 4 hours on low or 1 to 2 hours on high.

While the chicken is cooking, prepare the noodles according to package directions and set aside.

Transfer the chicken to a cutting board and shred or cut into cubes, then toss back into the slow cooker. Stir in the bok choy, red pepper, carrots and noodles. To thicken the sauce, whisk together the cornstarch and water in a small bowl and stir into the slow cooker. Allow the sauce to cook and thicken up on high for 30 minutes. Give everything a good stir to combine.

Serve hot and garnish with sesame seeds, if desired.

GENERAL TSO'S CHICKEN

This is one of my husband's favorite dishes that he orders every time we get takeout. Pan-frying the chicken on the stove beforehand adds an extra layer of crispiness we all love. The juicy bite-sized pieces are coated in a sweet, spicy and tangy sauce that is so good you can't help but wander back for seconds.

YIELD: 4 SERVINGS

¾ cup plus 1 tbsp (104 g) cornstarch, divided

¼ tsp black pepper

1½ lb (683 g) boneless, skinless chicken thighs or breasts, cut into bite-sized cubes

2 tsp (10 ml) cooking oil

1 cup (237 ml) low sodium soy sauce

½ cup (118 ml) water

4 tbsp (84 g) honey

2 tbsp (32 g) hoisin sauce

1½ tbsp (22 ml) apple cider vinegar

2 tbsp (32 g) ketchup or tomato paste

½ tsp fish sauce

½ tsp sesame oil

3 garlic cloves, minced

1 tsp fresh ginger, minced

3–4 tsp (48–64 g) red chili garlic paste, to taste

4–5 dried red chilies, or to taste

2 tbsp (30 ml) chilled water

Cooked rice, for serving

1 green onion, thinly sliced, for garnish (optional)

Sesame seeds, for garnish (optional)

In a large zip-top bag, toss together ¾ cup (95 g) cornstarch and black pepper. Next add the chicken to the bag, and give it a little shake until well coated.

In a large skillet, heat the oil over medium-high heat. Cook the chicken, about 2 to 3 minutes on both sides, then transfer to the slow cooker.

In a medium bowl, whisk together the soy sauce, water, honey, hoisin sauce, vinegar, ketchup, fish sauce, sesame oil, garlic, ginger and chili paste and pour over the chicken. Cover and cook on low for about 3 to 4 hours.

About 30 minutes prior to serving, toss in the dried chilies, then whisk together the remaining cornstarch with water in a small bowl and stir into the slow cooker. Turn heat to high and allow the sauce to cook and thicken up for about 20 to 30 minutes.

Serve with cooked rice and garnish with green onions and sesame seeds, if desired.

KOREAN-STYLE SHORT RIBS (GALBI)

My husband and I were lucky enough that we used to live in a city where great Korean food was plentiful. We had a few favorite places that we would frequent at least twice a month, where my husband would get his fix of Korean-Style Short Ribs. They are juicy, flavorful and cooked in a savory and tangy sauce. The soda adds the right amount of sweetness while also helping to tenderize the meat.

YIELD: 4 SERVINGS

¾ cup (177 ml) low sodium soy sauce

½ cup (118 ml) beef broth

¼ cup (59 ml) 7Up or Sprite

2 tbsp (25 g) brown sugar

1 tbsp (15 ml) rice wine vinegar

1 tbsp (15 ml) sesame oil

¼ tsp red pepper chili flakes

4 garlic cloves

½" (1.3-cm) piece of fresh ginger

1 Asian or Bosc pear, peeled, cored and cut into large chunks

½ tsp salt

½ tsp black pepper

2 tsp (10 ml) cooking oil

4 lb (1815 g) Korean-style beef short ribs (beef chuck flanken, cut ⅓–½" [8.5–12.7 mm])

½ cup (75 g) carrots, chopped into 1" (2.5-cm) pieces

½ cup (60 g) daikon radish, cubed

Cooked rice, for serving

1 green onion, sliced thinly, for garnish (optional)

Sesame seeds, for garnish (optional)

Add the soy sauce, broth, 7Up, sugar, vinegar, sesame oil, chili flakes, garlic, ginger and pear to a blender and purée until smooth.

Season the ribs with salt and pepper. In a large skillet, heat the oil over medium-high heat. Sear the ribs until just brown, about 1 to 2 minutes on both sides then transfer to a 5- to 6-quart (4.7- to 5.7-L) slow cooker. Add carrots and daikon to the slow cooker then cover with sauce. Place the lid on top and cook on low for 6 to 7 hours or on high for 3 to 4 hours, until the beef is tender, skimming off any excess fat.

Serve with cooked rice along with any extra sauce, and garnish with green onions and sesame seeds, if desired.

> **NOTE:** Korean-style beef short ribs can be found at most Asian markets. They are a thin strip of meat, since they are cut lengthwise across the rib bones.

KUNG PAO CHICKEN

Kung Pao chicken is a classic Szechuan dish stir-fried in a spicy, sweet and savory sauce.
We had this popular takeout dish often during our trip to China a few years ago and I love how simple
it is to customize at home. We'll usually tone down the spices when we are making this for the kids,
so feel free to adjust the amount of heat according to your taste.

YIELD: 4 SERVINGS

¾ cup plus 1½ tbsp (108 g) cornstarch

¼ tsp black pepper

1½ lb (683 g) boneless, skinless chicken thighs or breasts, cut into bite-sized cubes

2 tsp (10 ml) cooking oil

½ cup (118 ml) low sodium soy sauce

⅓ cup (79 ml) water

⅓ cup (79 ml) Chinese black vinegar or balsamic vinegar

3 tbsp (63 g) honey

2 tbsp (32 g) hoisin sauce

1 tsp sesame oil

3 garlic cloves, minced

1 tsp fresh ginger, minced

¼–½ tsp ground Sichuan peppercorn or red pepper chili flakes, to taste

3 tbsp (45 ml) cool water

4–6 dried red chili peppers, to taste

1 green bell pepper, chopped into 1" (2.5-cm) chunks

⅔ cup (100 g) unsalted cashews, roasted

Cooked rice, for serving

1 green onion, thinly sliced, for garnish (optional)

Sesame seeds, for garnish (optional)

In a large zip-top bag, toss together ¾ cup (95 g) cornstarch and black pepper. Next add the chicken to the bag, and give it a little shake until well coated.

In a large skillet, heat the oil over medium-high heat. Cook the chicken, about 2 to 3 minutes on both sides, and then transfer to the slow cooker.

In a medium bowl, whisk together the soy sauce, water, vinegar, honey, hoisin sauce, sesame oil, garlic, ginger and peppercorn and pour over the chicken. Cover and cook on low for about 3 to 4 hours.

About 30 minutes prior to serving, whisk together the remaining cornstarch with water in a small bowl and stir into the slow cooker. Toss in the dried red chili peppers, bell pepper and cashews, stirring to combine. Turn the heat to high and allow the sauce to cook and thicken up for about 20 to 30 minutes.

Serve hot over rice. Garnish with green onions and sesame seeds, if desired.

SPICY MONGOLIAN BEEF AND PINEAPPLE

It was always a treat for us when our parents would take us downtown to this fancy Chinese restaurant for special occasions. We got to dress up and ogle the shiny gold dragon statues that adorned the back wall and their pretty white and gold tablecloths. One of the dishes we would always order was Mongolian beef, a popular Chinese-American takeout dish. For my version, I like to add pineapples along with a touch of sweet red chili sauce and chili flakes for some extra heat.

YIELD: 4 SERVINGS

½ cup plus 1½ tbsp (78 g) cornstarch, divided

1 tsp baking soda (optional)

¼ tsp salt

¼ tsp black pepper

2 tsp (10 ml) cooking oil

1½ lb (683 g) flank steak, cut across the grain into thin strips

½ cup (118 ml) low sodium soy sauce

⅔ cup (158 ml) low sodium beef broth

⅓ cup (65 g) brown sugar, packed

2 tbsp (32 g) hoisin sauce

1 tbsp (16 g) Thai sweet red chili sauce

¼–½ tsp red pepper chili flakes, to taste

2 garlic cloves, minced

1 tsp fresh ginger, thinly sliced

2 tbsp (30 ml) cool water

½ cup (110 g) shredded or matchstick carrots

1 cup (180 g) pineapple chunks (fresh or canned)

¼ cup (59 ml) pineapple juice

Cooked rice, for serving

2 green onions, sliced thinly, for garnish (optional)

Sesame seeds, for garnish (optional)

In a large zip-top bag, toss together ½ cup (65 g) cornstarch, baking soda, salt and black pepper. Add the beef to the bag and give it a little shake until well coated.

In a large skillet, heat the oil over medium-high heat. Sear the beef for about 1 to 2 minutes on both sides and add to the slow cooker.

In a medium bowl, whisk together the soy sauce, broth, sugar, hoisin sauce, chili sauce, chili flakes, garlic and ginger until dissolved and pour over the beef. Cover with the lid and cook on low for about 3 to 4 hours.

About 30 minutes prior to serving, whisk together the remaining cornstarch with water in a small bowl and stir into the slow cooker along with the carrots, pineapples and pineapple juice. Cover with the lid, then turn the heat to high and allow the sauce to cook and thicken up for about 20 to 30 minutes.

Serve over cooked rice and garnish with green onions and sesame seeds, if desired.

SWEET AND SOUR CHICKEN

When I was younger, sweet and sour anything was one of my favorite flavors and anytime my mom made it, my brothers and I would rush to help set the table. Here, tender bite-sized chicken, sweet pineapples and crunchy bell peppers get a generous coating of the sweet and tangy sauce. This is a lighter version of the classic Cantonese dish but is just as delicious!

YIELD: 4 SERVINGS

. . . .

1 cup plus 1½ tbsp (140 g) cornstarch

¼ tsp black pepper

1½ lb (683 g) boneless, skinless chicken thighs or breasts, cut into bite-sized cubes

2 tsp (10 ml) cooking oil

½ cup (118 ml) low sodium soy sauce

¼ cup (59 ml) low sodium chicken broth

3 tbsp (37 g) brown sugar or honey (63 g)

3 tbsp (48 g) tomato paste or ketchup

1½ tbsp (22 ml) apple cider vinegar

2 tsp (10 g) oyster sauce

1 tsp dark soy sauce (leave out if you can't find this)

¼ tsp sesame oil

2 garlic cloves, minced

½ tsp fresh ginger, minced

2 tbsp (30 ml) cool water

1 cup (165 g) pineapple, cut into bite-sized chunks (fresh or frozen)

2 red bell peppers, cut into 1" (2.5-cm) pieces

Cooked rice, for serving

Sesame seeds, for garnish (optional)

1 green onion, thinly sliced, for garnish (optional)

In a large zip-top bag, toss together 1 cup (125 g) cornstarch and black pepper. Add the chicken to the bag and give it a little shake until well coated.

In a large skillet, heat the oil over medium-high heat. Add the chicken and cook for about 1 to 2 minutes on each side, and then transfer to the slow cooker.

In a medium bowl, whisk together the soy sauce, broth, sugar, tomato paste, vinegar, oyster sauce, dark soy sauce, sesame oil, garlic and ginger and pour over the chicken. Cook on low for about 3 to 4 hours.

About 30 minutes prior to serving, whisk together the remaining cornstarch with water in a small bowl and stir into the slow cooker along with the pineapple and bell peppers. Turn the heat to high and allow the sauce to cook and thicken up for about 20 to 30 minutes.

Serve with cooked rice and sprinkle with sesame seeds and green onions, if desired.

TERIYAKI CHICKEN WITH SOBA NOODLES

Teriyaki chicken was one of the very first Japanese dishes I tried back when I was in high school. With the glossy, sweet and savory sauce—it was love at first bite for me. This version comes together easily by just tossing all the ingredients into the slow cooker. Serving it over buckwheat soba noodles makes it a delicious and satisfying meal.

YIELD: 4 SERVINGS

2 boneless, skinless chicken breast halves, split in half (820 g)

½ cup plus 2 tbsp (148 ml) low sodium soy sauce, divided

⅓ cup plus 2 tbsp (156 g) honey, divided

¼ cup plus 1 tbsp (74 ml) rice wine vinegar, divided

2 tbsp (30 ml) mirin

1 tbsp (15 ml) sake, Chinese rice wine or dry sherry

2 garlic cloves, minced

2 tsp (3 g) minced fresh ginger

1 tbsp (9 g) cornstarch

2 tbsp (30 ml) cold water

6 oz (170 g) dried buckwheat soba noodles

1 tsp sesame oil

Cooked, shelled edamame beans, for serving (optional)

2 green onions, thinly sliced, for garnish (optional)

Sesame seeds, for garnish (optional)

Combine the chicken, ½ cup (118 ml) soy sauce, ⅓ cup (113 g) honey, ¼ cup (59 ml) vinegar, mirin, sake, garlic and ginger in the bottom of the slow cooker. Cook on low for 4 to 6 hours. Transfer each chicken piece to a cutting board and cut into strips.

To thicken the sauce, whisk together the cornstarch and water in a small bowl and stir into the slow cooker along with the chicken strips. Allow the sauce to cook and thicken up for about 20 to 30 minutes.

Meanwhile, prepare the soba noodles according to package directions and drain. In a large mixing bowl, whisk together the remaining soy sauce, honey, vinegar and the sesame oil and combine with the noodles, tossing until well coated.

Serve in individual bowls with chicken and edamame beans, if using. Spoon additional sauce over the chicken and sprinkle with sliced green onions and sesame seeds, if desired.

THAI RED CURRY PEANUT CHICKEN

Thai food makes my heart sing and belly smile. I could have it for breakfast, lunch or dinner every day so it was a dream come true for my taste buds when I had a chance to visit Thailand a few years ago. This recipe is an adapted version of a dish we had often during our visit. The rich peanut sauce has all the signature Thai flavors with layers of sweet, salty, sour and spicy in every magical bite.

YIELD: 4 SERVINGS

1 medium onion, thinly sliced

2 lb (910 g) boneless, skinless chicken thighs or chicken breasts cut into 1" (2.5-cm) chunks

1 red bell pepper, chopped into 1" (2.5-cm) chunks

1 cup (237 ml) low sodium chicken broth

⅓ cup (85 g) natural peanut butter

2 tbsp (42 g) honey

2 tbsp (32 g) red curry paste

1 tbsp (15 ml) fish sauce

3 garlic cloves, minced

½ tbsp (7 g) minced fresh ginger

1 cup (237 ml) canned coconut milk

2 cups (250 g) broccoli florets

Cooked rice, for serving

½ cup (25 g) chopped fresh cilantro, for serving (optional)

1 tbsp (14 g) chopped roasted peanuts, for serving (optional)

Place the onion slices in the bottom of the slow cooker followed by the chicken and red peppers. In a small bowl, whisk together the broth, peanut butter, honey, curry paste, fish sauce, garlic and ginger and pour evenly over the chicken.

Cook on low for 5 to 6 hours or on high for 2 to 3 hours. Stir in the coconut milk and broccoli and cook on high for an additional 25 to 30 minutes, or until the broccoli is tender.

Divide into bowls and serve with rice. Garnish with cilantro and peanuts, if desired.

5 Ingredients or Less

How many times does it feel like there just aren't enough hours in the day? Recipes that use a handful of ingredients are perfect for those busy nights when you don't have time to measure or chop a million things.

This chapter is full of 5-ingredient recipes that you can serve alone or along with the optional sides and garnishes as noted. You can get dinner on the table with little effort and without sacrificing on flavor. Fill your dinner menu with these simple recipes that will fit every family's tastes!

CHILI ORANGE BEEF

This is an easy and versatile beef dish for those nights when you want something tasty without a lot of effort. It takes less than 10 minutes of prep time and you can serve it as a filler in sandwiches, in tacos or over a bed of cooked rice. The spicy, sweet and tangy sauce is made with just 4 ingredients that you'll want to reach for again and again.

YIELD: 4 SERVINGS

⅔ cup (158 ml) Thai sweet chili sauce

¼ cup (59 ml) orange juice or orange marmalade

2 tbsp (32 g) oyster sauce

⅛ tsp five-spice powder

1½ lb (683 g) flank steak, skirt steak or sirloin, cut into thin ¼" (6-mm) strips

Cooked rice, for serving

Sesame seeds, for garnish (optional)

In a medium bowl, combine the chili sauce, orange juice, oyster sauce and five-spice powder. Add the beef to the bottom of the slow cooker and pour the sauce over the top. Cook on low for 3 to 4 hours.

Serve with cooked rice and sprinkle with sesame seeds, if desired.

CHINESE FIVE-SPICE PORK TENDERLOIN

This pork tenderloin is an easy version of the popular Chinese BBQ pork typically found in Cantonese restaurants and butchers. The sweet and smoky sauce comes together with just four ingredients, making this meal perfect for any night you need a tasty and stress-free meal. Serve it with some steamed rice and a medley of vegetables for a complete dinner.

YIELD: 4–6 SERVINGS

3 lb (1360 g) pork tenderloin

½ cup (100 g) dark brown sugar

4 tbsp (60 g) hoisin sauce

4 tbsp (60 ml) low sodium soy sauce

2 tsp (10 ml) five-spice powder

Cooked rice, for serving

1 green onion, sliced thinly, for garnish (optional)

Lay a large piece of aluminum foil on a large plate and place the pork in the center.

In a small bowl, mix together the brown sugar, hoisin sauce, soy sauce and five-spice powder and spread evenly on both sides of the pork. Fold the foil over the top and crimp the sides to close. Marinate in the fridge for at least 2 hours. When ready to cook, place the foil packet into the bottom of a slow cooker and cook on low for 4 to 6 hours.

Slice into rounds and serve with cooked rice and sprinkle with green onion, if desired.

EASY SHORTCUT FRIED RICE

Fried rice was a staple when we were growing up. It was my mom's way of using up any leftover veggies we had hanging around in the fridge. This slow-cooker version may not be traditional but it couldn't be simpler to put together if you already have day-old rice on hand. Just toss everything into the slow cooker along with some seasoning and you have an easy and tasty lunch or dinner side dish that you can serve with any protein of your choice.

YIELD: 4 SERVINGS

3 cups (525 g) cooked, day-old rice (I recommend using jasmine rice)

1 cup (150 g) fresh or frozen chopped mixed vegetables

2 tbsp (30 ml) low sodium soy sauce

1 tbsp (15 ml) fish sauce

1 tbsp (15 ml) mirin

Add the rice and vegetables into a 4- to 5-quart (3.8- to 4.7-L) slow cooker. Stir in the soy sauce, fish sauce and mirin. Cover and cook on high for 1 hour or low for 3 hours. Stir well before serving.

GINGER-GLAZED COD

We eat a lot of fish in our house and white fish is a favorite with our kids. The mild taste pairs wonderfully with the tangy balsamic and ginger glaze. It's a light, flavorful dish and with the easy foil packets, clean-up is a breeze!

YIELD: 4 SERVINGS

3 tbsp (45 ml) balsamic vinegar

3 tbsp (63 g) honey

2½ tbsp (38 ml) low sodium soy sauce

2 tsp grated fresh ginger

4 (4-oz [400-g]) cod or any white fish fillets

Cooked rice, for serving

Chopped fresh cilantro, for garnish (optional)

Sesame seeds for garnish (optional)

In a small mixing bowl, whisk together balsamic vinegar, honey, soy sauce and ginger until combined. In a large resealable container, lay four sheets of aluminum foil and place each fillet inside. Brush or spoon the glaze over each fillet and wrap all sides of the foil to cover and seal closed. Cover with the lid and let marinate in the fridge for at least 3 hours or overnight.

When ready to cook, place the foil packets into the slow cooker. Cook on high for 2 hours, or until the fish flakes easily with a fork.

Serve hot with additional glaze alongside cooked rice and sprinkle with cilantro and sesame seeds, if desired.

NOTE: For a crispy crust, place fillets under broiler for 2 to 3 minutes.

GREEN CURRY LEMONGRASS CHICKEN

Green curry is a recipe I often turn to whenever I'm craving a comforting dish with a kick of heat. This easy version uses ready-made green curry paste and comes together with minimal ingredients while still packing an aromatic and flavorful punch. It's fresh, fragrant and leaves you feeling warm and cozy inside.

YIELD: 4 SERVINGS

1 (14-oz [392-g]) can coconut milk

3 tbsp (48 g) green curry paste

2 stalks lemongrass, stalks removed and white portion sliced thinly

2 tsp (10 ml) fish sauce

2 lb (910 g) skinless, boneless chicken thighs or chicken breasts, cut into 1" (2.5-cm) chunks

Cooked rice, for serving

Fresh chopped cilantro and Thai basil, for garnish (optional)

In the bottom of a 4-quart (3.8-L) slow cooker, mix together the coconut milk, green curry paste, lemongrass and fish sauce. Place the chicken on top and coat with the sauce. Cook on low for 4 to 5 hours.

Serve with cooked rice and garnish with cilantro and Thai basil, if desired.

PINEAPPLE TERIYAKI BEEF

Teriyaki Beef is one of my husband's favorite Japanese takeout dishes. After I showed him an easier semi-homemade version in the slow cooker, he now makes it whenever that craving hits. Tender beef strips are slow cooked with sweet pineapples and a tangy, savory sauce. It's a satisfying meal that the entire family will love.

YIELD: 6 SERVINGS

8 oz (225 g) canned pineapple chunks, juice drained and reserved

⅓ cup (79 ml) low sodium soy sauce

¼ cup (55 g) hoisin sauce

¼ cup (59 ml) mirin

2 lb (910 g) flank, top or sirloin steak, cut very thinly across the grain in strips

Cooked rice, for serving

1 green onion, thinly sliced, for garnish (optional)

Sesame seeds, for garnish (optional)

In a 4- to 6-quart (3.8- to 5.7-L) slow cooker, mix together the pineapple juice, soy sauce, hoisin sauce and mirin until combined. Toss in the steak and coat evenly with the sauce. Cook on low for 4 to 6 hours or on high for 2 to 4 hours. Remove the lid and stir in the pineapples and cook on high for 20 minutes.

Serve with cooked rice with sliced green onions and sesame seeds, if desired.

NOTE: For a thicker sauce, make a cornstarch slurry of 1 tablespoon (9 g) of cornstarch whisked into 2 tablespoons (30 ml) cold water and add it to the slow cooker when stirring in the pineapples.

SRIRACHA CHILI CHICKEN WINGS

Wings are a popular choice in our home, especially when they are covered in a sticky, sweet and spicy sauce. They make great party appetizers or a fun and tasty weeknight meal. To give them a slightly crispy coating, I like to finish them under the broiler which also helps to seal in the flavor.

YIELD: 4 SERVINGS

½ cup (170 g) honey

5 tbsp (70 g) butter, melted

3 tbsp (44 ml) Sriracha

3 tsp (15 g) Thai sweet chili sauce

3 lb (1350 g) chicken wings, cut into drumettes, tips removed

Chopped fresh cilantro, for garnish (optional)

Sesame seeds, for garnish (optional)

Mix together the honey, melted butter, Sriracha and sweet chili sauce in the bottom of a 5- to 6-quart (4.7- to 5.7-L) slow cooker. Add the wings and toss to coat evenly.

Cook on low for 4 to 5 hours or on high for 2 to 3 hours, watching near the end, until the meat is tender but not falling off the bones.

Gently transfer the wings to a foil-lined baking sheet in a single layer. Brush the wings with some of the sauce in the slow cooker and broil for 5 minutes, flipping once and topping with more sauce. Remove from the oven and garnish with cilantro and sesame seeds, if desired.

NOTE: Broiling helps to add crispiness to the wings and seal in the flavors but if you're in a hurry, feel free to skip this step.

SWEET CHILI CHICKEN DRUMSTICKS

My kids get excited every time drumsticks are on our dinner menu. They love picking them up with their hands and getting a little messy. These cook up nice and tender in the slow cooker and are coated in a sweet, spicy and perfectly addicting sticky glaze.

YIELD: 4-6 SERVINGS

⅔ cup (158 ml) low sodium soy sauce

⅔ cup (150 g) Thai sweet chili sauce

2 tsp (10 ml) fish sauce

2" (5-cm) fresh ginger root, minced

4 to 5 lb (1.8 to 2.3 kg) chicken drumsticks

Fresh chopped cilantro, for garnish (optional)

Sesame seeds, for garnish (optional)

In a large resealable container, combine the soy sauce, sweet chili sauce, fish sauce and ginger. Place the chicken on top and toss to coat well. Place it in the fridge and allow the chicken to marinate for at least 3 hours or overnight. When ready to cook, dump the chicken and marinade into the bottom of a 6-quart (5.7-L) slow cooker. Cook on low for 5 to 6 hours or on high for 3 to 4 hours.

Carefully transfer the drumsticks to a foil-lined baking sheet. Brush with any extra sauce remaining and broil on high for 3 minutes on each side, flipping once and coating with more sauce. Remove from the oven and garnish with cilantro and sesame seeds, if desired.

NOTE: Broiling helps to add crispiness to the drumsticks and seal in the flavors but if you're in a hurry, feel free to skip this step.

SWEET AND SOUR SHRIMP WITH PINEAPPLES

My kids love anything with pineapples so this is an easy meal we make often during the week. The juicy shrimp pairs beautifully with the sweet and tangy pineapples and crispy bell peppers. It's super simple and lets you enjoy this popular takeout dish without having to leave your home.

YIELD: 4 SERVINGS

1½ lb (185 g) uncooked jumbo shrimp, peeled and deveined

3 bell peppers (preferably tricolored package), seeded and cut into large chunks

2 red onions, cut into large chunks

1 (20-oz [475-g]) can pineapple chunks, drained

2 cups (450 g) ready-made sweet and sour sauce

Cooked noodles, for serving (optional)

1 green onion, thinly sliced, for garnish (optional)

Sesame seeds, for garnish (optional)

Add the shrimp, bell peppers, onions and pineapple chunks into the bottom of the slow cooker. Pour sweet and sour sauce evenly over everything and toss to coat well.

Cook on high for 2 to 3 hours, or until the shrimp is fully cooked and the vegetables have softened.

Serve with some cooked noodles and sprinkle with green onions and sesame seeds, if desired.

THAI PUMPKIN CURRY SOUP

I adore pumpkin all year long. It's a healthy and versatile ingredient and adds a smooth and creamy texture when blended into soups. This cozy soup is a great dish to make once the weather cools down. It comes together easily with minimal ingredients. Sweet coconut and red curry paste make it a comforting addition to chilly fall days.

YIELD: 6 SERVINGS

4 cups (900 g) pure pumpkin purée (fresh or canned)

3½ cups (828 ml) low sodium chicken or vegetable broth

1½ tbsp (12 g) red curry paste

½ tsp garlic powder

1 (13.5-oz [400-ml]) can coconut milk, reserving 1–2 tbsp (15–30 ml) for garnish

Pumpkin seeds, for garnish (optional)

In a 5- to 6-quart (4.7- to 5.7-L) slow cooker, stir in the pumpkin purée, chicken broth, red curry paste and garlic powder until combined. Cook on low for 4 to 5 hours or high for 2 to 3 hours. Stir in the coconut milk and cook on high for 20 minutes, or until heated through.

Serve warm in bowls and garnish with reserved coconut milk and pumpkin seeds, if desired.

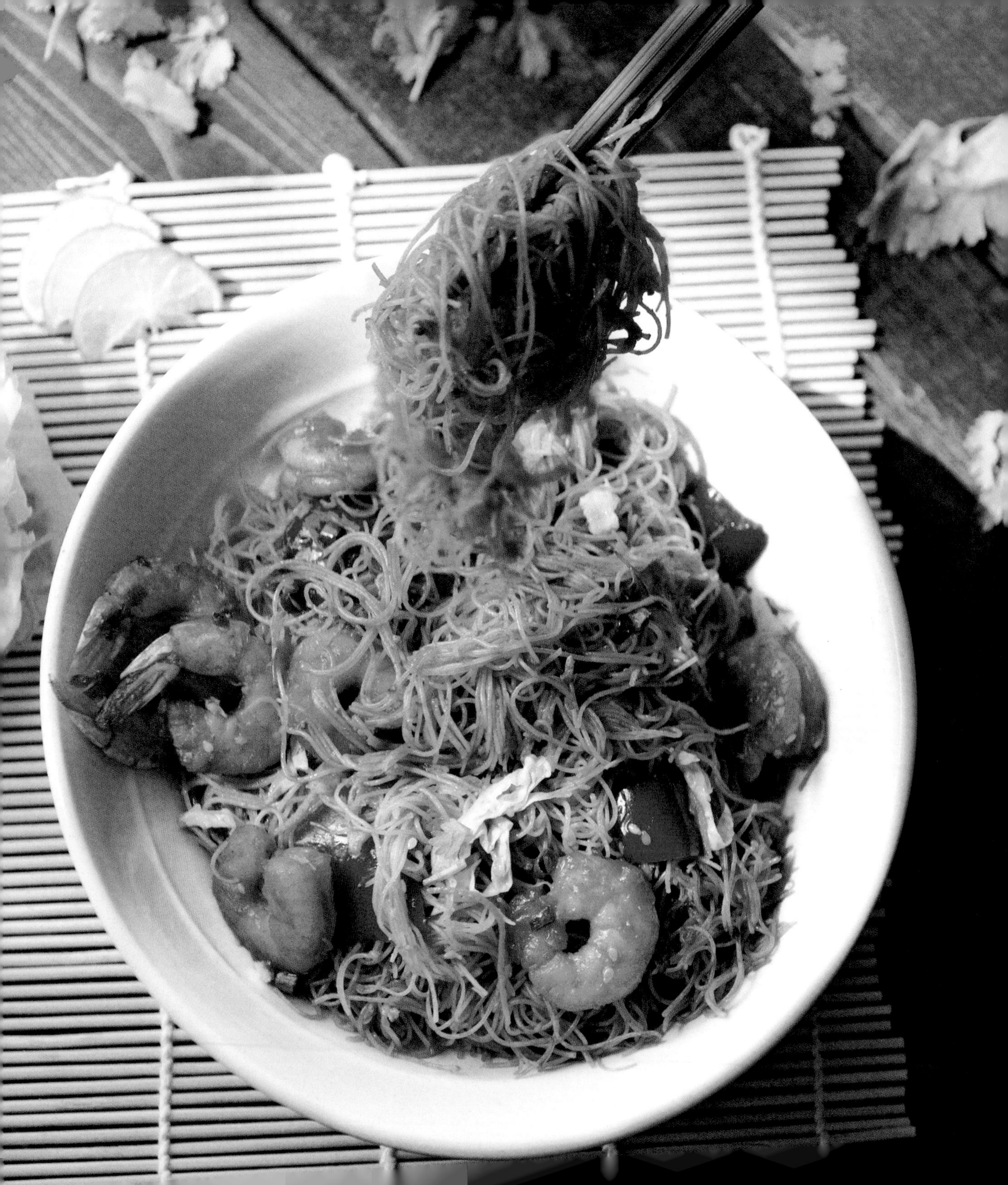

One-Pot & Skillet Meals

Do you ever have those evenings when 5 o'clock rolls around and you haven't even thought about what to make for dinner yet? It happens frequently around here with two active young kids. That's when these easy one-pot wonders come to the rescue!

Along with slow-cooker meals, skillet and one-pot wonders are a staple in our home. They are fast, easy and the perfect solution to weeknight craziness! Clean up is a breeze with only one pan to wash, which works out for me because washing dishes is my least favorite chore. Just toss a bunch of ingredients into your pan and watch them come together to make a delicious meal! Many of these can be made in 30 minutes or less. What could be a better dinner solution? Just grab a fork and dig into these easy skillet meals!

BEEF CHOW FUN
STIR-FRIED RICE NOODLES

Beef Chow Fun is my all-time favorite Cantonese dish. It's made by stir-frying rice noodles with tender slices of beef, fragrant scallions and crunchy bean sprouts. What makes these comforting noodles so popular is the infamous smoky char aka "wok hei," which adds depth and umami to this sweet and savory dish. Fresh rice noodles from the Asian market work best but you can use dried rice noodles in a pinch.

YIELD: 4 SERVINGS

· ·

12 oz (340 g) fresh flat "ho fun" rice noodles or 8 oz (226 g) dried wide rice noodles, prepared according to package instructions

1 tsp sesame oil, divided

2 tbsp (30 ml) dark soy sauce

2 tbsp (30 ml) low sodium soy sauce

½ tbsp (8 g) oyster sauce

½ tbsp (8 ml) Chinese cooking wine (Shaoxing) or dry sherry

½ tsp cornstarch

½ tsp brown sugar

¼ tsp salt

¼ tsp black pepper

Pinch of ground white pepper

8 oz (228 g) flank steak, sliced thinly across the grain

4 tsp (20 ml) cooking oil, divided

2 tsp minced fresh ginger

3 garlic cloves, minced

1 medium onion, thinly sliced

4 green onions, split in half vertically and sliced into 2" (5-cm) pieces

1 cup (100 g) fresh mung bean sprouts, washed & dried

Sesame seeds, for garnish (optional)

In a large bowl, separate the fresh noodle strands and lightly coat with ½ teaspoon sesame oil. This helps the noodles not to stick when stir-frying them in the pan.

In a medium bowl, whisk together the soy sauces, oyster sauce, wine, cornstarch, sugar, ½ teaspoon sesame oil, salt and pepper for the sauce and marinade. Toss the beef with one-third of the sauce mixture in another medium bowl while reserving the remaining sauce for the noodles. Marinate the beef for at least 30 minutes.

Heat a non-stick skillet or wok over high heat and swirl in 2 teaspoons (10 ml) of oil. Sear the beef for 1 minute, on both sides, then transfer to a plate and set aside.

Return the same skillet back to the stove, give it a quick wipe with a cloth and add another 2 teaspoons (10 ml) of oil. Toss in the ginger and allow to sit for 5 to 10 seconds, then add garlic, onion and green onions. Quickly stir-fry for 20 seconds, until fragrant.

Spread the noodles evenly out in the skillet and toss to combine using tongs or chopsticks. Add the remaining sauce and beef slices back, then give everything a quick toss using tongs. Add the bean sprouts and stir-fry for an additional 2 to 3 minutes, until the sauce has thickened and everything is heated through and combined. Remove from the heat and serve immediately. Sprinkle with sesame seeds and additional green onions, if desired.

CHICKEN ADOBO WITH COCONUT LIME RICE

This traditional Filipino dish is a simple and comforting meal that has the same flavors of something my mom used to make for us when we were younger. Tender and juicy chicken gets braised in a sweet and tangy vinegar sauce balanced out by the creamy coconut rice. It's an easy weeknight meal that cooks up in just one pot.

YIELD: 4 SERVINGS

⅓ cup (79 ml) apple cider vinegar

¼ cup (59 ml) low sodium soy sauce

2 tsp (14 g) honey

1 tsp whole black peppercorns

3 dried bay leaves

4 garlic cloves, minced

1½–2 lb (685–910 g) boneless, skinless chicken thighs

2 tsp (10 ml) cooking oil

2 green onions, thinly sliced, plus more for garnish

1 tbsp (16 g) cornstarch

2¼ cups (530 ml) water, divided

2 cups (370 g) white rice, rinsed

1¾ cups (414 ml) canned coconut milk

1 tsp lime zest

½ tsp salt

⅓ cup (15 g) chopped fresh cilantro, divided

Sesame seeds, for garnish

In a large container, combine the vinegar, soy sauce, honey, peppercorns, bay leaves and garlic for the marinade. Reserve half of the sauce and set aside. Add the chicken to the container and toss well to combine. Store in the fridge for at least 2 hours for the flavors to meld together.

In a large heavy pot, heat the oil over medium-high heat. Add the chicken and cook until lightly browned, around 4 to 5 minutes on each side. Add the onions and sauté for another 2 to 3 minutes, until fragrant and the onions have softened. Whisk together the cornstarch with the reserved sauce plus ¼ cup (59 ml) water and pour into the pot. Bring to a boil and allow the sauce to thicken. Transfer the chicken and sauce to a large platter and set aside.

In the same pot over medium-high heat, add the rinsed rice, 2 cups (480 ml) water, coconut milk, lime zest and salt. Bring the mixture to a boil, stirring once or twice to avoid sticking. Turn the heat down to low then cover with the lid. Cook for another 10 minutes then give it a good stir.

Return the chicken back to the pot, nestling on top of the rice. Add 2 tablespoons (30 ml) of sauce over each chicken piece. Cover with the lid once again and continue to cook for an additional 10 to 15 minutes, or until the rice and chicken are cooked through. Stir in half of the cilantro and top with more sauce as needed.

Divide onto plates and serve garnished with green onions, sesame seeds and remaining cilantro, if desired.

CHICKEN CHOW MEIN

Chow Mein was a favorite of mine growing up. My mom would make these classic stir-fried noodles for us whenever she had leftover veggies and meat she wanted to use up. They are quick, easy and make a delicious clean-out-the-fridge meal all without having to order takeout!

YIELD: 4 SERVINGS

8 oz (226 g) fresh egg noodles or cooked chow mein or ramen noodles

1½ tbsp (24 g) oyster sauce

½ tbsp (7 ml) low sodium soy sauce

1 tsp honey or brown sugar

¾ tsp cornstarch

¼ tsp sesame oil

⅓ cup (79 ml) low sodium chicken broth or water

⅛ tsp ground white pepper

Salt and black pepper to taste

½ lb (226 g) skinless, boneless chicken breast, cut into 1″ (2.5-cm) chunks

1 tbsp (14 ml) cooking oil, divided

3 garlic cloves, minced

½ tsp minced fresh ginger

2 cups (200 g) shredded Napa cabbage, washed and dried

¼ cup (55 g) shredded carrots

½ cup (110 g) mung bean sprouts, rinsed and drained

2 green onions (cut into 2″ [5-cm] length)

Sesame seeds, for garnish (optional)

Prepare the noodles according to package instructions.

In a medium bowl, whisk together the oyster sauce, soy sauce, honey, cornstarch, sesame oil, broth, white pepper, salt and black pepper for the sauce until evenly combined. Measure out 2 tablespoons (30 ml) and pour over the chicken in a separate bowl, reserving the remaining sauce for the noodles. Marinate the chicken for at least 30 minutes.

In a large skillet or wok, heat 1 teaspoon of oil over medium-high heat. Add the chicken and sauté for 2 to 3 minutes on each side, until browned. Remove the chicken from the pan and set aside on a plate. Wipe down the pan with a cloth and return back to medium-high heat. Swirl in 2 teaspoons (10 ml) of oil. Then, add the garlic and ginger and stir-fry until fragrant, for about 30 seconds. Toss in the cabbage and carrots and cook for another 1 to 2 minutes, or until just starting to wilt.

Add the noodles, then give the reserved sauce a quick stir and pour into the pan. Toss the noodles continuously to coat with sauce and allow to boil. Adjust seasonings and add more water to thin out the sauce, if desired.

Stir in the bean sprouts and green onions while quickly tossing for about 30 seconds to a minute, until all the ingredients are combined and heated through. Serve hot topped with sesame seeds, if desired.

CLASSIC FRIED RICE

Fried rice is the ultimate comfort food for me and the very first "from scratch" dish I ever learned how to make. It's the one dish that still shows up on our dinner table the most. You can use up leftover rice, veggies and protein to come up with different variations. Using cold, day-old rice is the secret to achieving restaurant-quality fried rice. If you're in a pinch and don't have any leftovers on hand, make a fresh batch using 25 percent less water than you normally would.

YIELD: 4 SERVINGS

1 cup (225 g) cubed lean beef, chicken or pork (leave out for meatless version)

1½ tbsp (23 ml) low sodium soy sauce, divided

½ tsp cornstarch

¼ tsp black pepper

1 tbsp (15 ml) cooking oil, divided

3 garlic cloves, finely minced

1 cup (150 g) frozen mixed vegetables

2 large eggs, lightly beaten

3 cups (555 g) cooked, day-old rice, chilled with clumps separated

1 tsp fish sauce OR 1 tbsp (10 g) oyster sauce (vegetarian or regular)

1 tsp mirin, Chinese cooking wine or dry sherry

¼ tsp sesame oil

Salt and black pepper, to taste

1 green onion, thinly sliced, for garnish (optional)

Sesame seeds, for garnish (optional)

In a small bowl, combine the meat with ½ tablespoon (8 ml) of soy sauce, cornstarch and black pepper.

Heat 2 teaspoons (10 ml) of cooking oil on medium-high heat in a non-stick wok or pan. Toss in the garlic and sauté until fragrant; about 10 seconds. Add the cubed meat and stir-fry until almost cooked through, around 2 to 3 minutes. Stir in the mixed vegetables and cook for another minute, then push all the ingredients to one side of the pan and pour in the beaten eggs. Scramble into small pieces and cook, then transfer the entire contents of the pan to a large plate.

Return the same pan to the stove and add another teaspoon of oil. Stir in the rice and break up any large chunks with a spatula while tossing until heated through, around 2 minutes. Add the plate of cooked meat and vegetables back to the pan and drizzle in the remaining soy sauce, fish sauce, mirin and sesame oil, tossing to combine everything evenly. Keep stirring the fried rice until slightly toasted, about 2 minutes. Add salt and black pepper to taste.

Transfer to bowls and serve hot. Garnish with green onions and sesame seeds, if desired.

INDONESIAN MIE GORENG FRIED NOODLES

This fiery and flavorful street-fare dish is extremely popular in Southeast Asia. Fresh egg noodles are pan-fried together with chicken, shrimp and bean sprouts. It's an easy dish to make once you have all your ingredients prepped and ready to go, making this a a great dish to use up any lingering produce in your fridge. The sweet and spicy combo makes this supremely tasty and satisfying.

YIELD: 4 SERVINGS

2 tbsp (32 g) ketchup

2 tbsp (32 g) red chili garlic paste

2 tbsp (32 g) oyster sauce

1 tsp dark soy sauce

1 tsp sugar

1 tsp Chinese cooking wine or dry sherry

⅛ tsp ground white pepper

2 tsp (10 ml) cooking oil

2 garlic cloves, minced

½ tsp minced fresh ginger

½ lb (228 g) boneless, skinless chicken thighs, cut into 1" (2.5-cm) chunks

6 medium-sized shrimp, peeled and deveined

1 cup (100 g) shredded cabbage

1 large egg, lightly beaten

6 oz (175 g) fresh yellow egg noodles or cooked ramen or spaghetti noodles

1 cup (100 g) bean sprouts, rinsed and drained

Green onions, thinly sliced

Crispy fried shallots

Lime wedges

Tomato wedges

Roasted crushed peanuts or cashews

In a medium bowl, combine the ketchup, garlic paste, oyster sauce, dark soy sauce, sugar, wine and white pepper and set aside.

In a large non-stick wok or pan, heat the oil over medium-high heat. Sauté the garlic and ginger for about 30 seconds, or until fragrant. Add the chicken and stir-fry for a minute before tossing in the shrimp. Cook until opaque and no longer pink, around 3 to 4 minutes, then stir in the cabbage. Push all the ingredients to one side of the pan, add the egg and quickly scramble. Toss in the noodles, using tongs to separate the strands. Then, pour the sauce over the top, and toss until everything is coated. Stir in the bean sprouts and add water as needed.

Remove from the heat and serve with green onions, fried shallots, lime, tomato wedges and roasted peanuts.

NOTE: Use 1½–2 tablespoons (22–30 ml) kecap manis (Indonesian sweet soy sauce) with 2 tablespoons (30 ml) water for an easy sauce alternative.

PAD THAI NOODLES WITH CHICKEN

Pad Thai is easily one of my all-time favorite dishes. I think I must have ordered a plate for dinner almost every day on my visit to Thailand many years ago. Tamarind, sweet chili and fish sauce are the marvelous trio of ingredients that give these noodles the unmistakable Thai flavors that we all love. Spicy, sour, salty, sweet and utterly delicious.

YIELD: 4 SERVINGS

• •

8 oz (225 g) dried rice noodles or linguine noodles

½ cup (118 ml) tamarind concentrate or paste

⅓ cup (75 g) Thai sweet chili sauce

3 tbsp (45 ml) fish sauce

2 tbsp (25 g) coconut sugar or brown sugar

3–4 tsp (15–20 g) red chili garlic paste, to taste

⅛ tsp ground white pepper

2 tsp (10 ml) cooking oil

½ lb (228 g) chicken breast, cut into 1" (2.5-cm) pieces

2 garlic cloves, minced

½ tbsp (8 g) of fresh ginger, minced

1 shallot, diced

1 carrot, cut into matchsticks

1 red bell pepper, thinly sliced

1 large egg, lightly beaten

Lime wedges

Chopped fresh cilantro

Mung bean sprouts

Chopped roasted peanuts

Sliced green onions

Sesame seeds

Place the noodles in a large heatproof bowl. Fill with enough boiling water to cover the noodles and set aside to soak for 10 to 12 minutes, or until the noodles have softened. Drain and use a fork to separate the strands.

Meanwhile, combine the tamarind paste, chili sauce, fish sauce, coconut sugar, chili paste and white pepper in a medium bowl. Set aside.

Heat a non-stick skillet or wok over medium-high heat. Swirl 2 teaspoons (10 ml) of oil into the pan and add chicken. Cook for 2 to 3 minutes on both sides, or until slightly browned. Add the garlic, ginger and shallot and stir until fragrant, about 30 seconds. Stir in the carrot and bell pepper and cook until crisp-tender, about 1–2 minutes. Push the vegetables to one side of the pan and add the beaten egg. Allow to cook, while crumbling into small pieces. Add the drained noodles then pour the sauce over the top. Toss with tongs to coat evenly and allow the sauce to simmer and thicken, about 1 minute. Squeeze the juice from 1 lime wedge and taste to adjust seasonings.

Remove from heat and serve on a large platter topped with cilantro, mung bean sprouts, roasted peanuts, green onions, sesame seeds and extra lime wedges on the side.

SHANGHAI NOODLES

We first had this local staple when we visited Shanghai a few years ago.
It's a simple pan-fried dish made with fresh, thick and chewy Shanghai-style noodles that are
coated in a rich and deliciously addictive sauce. It's a favorite with my family as well
as my readers and makes a tasty meal for any night of the week.

YIELD: 4 SERVINGS

½–1 lb (228–453 g) extra-lean ground pork

¼ tsp salt

¼ tsp black pepper

2 tbsp (30 ml) water

1½ tbsp (22 ml) low sodium soy sauce

½ tbsp (8 ml) sesame oil

½ tbsp (8 ml) dark soy sauce

½ tbsp (8 g) oyster sauce

2 tsp (10 ml) Chinese cooking wine or dry sherry

1 tsp brown sugar

⅛ tsp ground white pepper

1 tbsp (9 g) cornstarch

¼ tsp Sriracha sauce or red pepper flakes, to taste (optional)

2 tsp (10 ml) cooking oil

2 garlic cloves, finely minced

1½ tbsp (12 g) grated fresh ginger

½ head Napa cabbage, thinly sliced

1 lb (453 g) fresh Shanghai-style noodles or Udon noodles

Sesame seeds, for garnish (optional)

In a medium bowl, season the ground pork with salt and pepper. In another small bowl, whisk together water, soy sauce, sesame oil, dark soy sauce, oyster sauce, wine, sugar, white pepper, cornstarch and Sriracha and set aside.

Heat the oil in a wok or heavy skillet on medium-high heat. Add garlic and ginger and sauté until fragrant, about 30 seconds. Crumble the ground pork, breaking up any large lumps, and cook until the meat is no longer pink, about 5 minutes. Mix in the cabbage and stir-fry until wilted, about 1 minute. Stir in noodles, breaking up strands if necessary and pour the sauce on top. Toss to coat evenly and until all the ingredients are combined.

Transfer to a serving platter and garnish with sesame seeds, if desired.

NOTE: If you can't find Shanghai noodles, you can substitute with cooked Udon or fettuccine noodles, prepared according to package directions.

SINGAPORE FRIED VERMICELLI RICE NOODLES

This is a popular Chinese takeout dish that we had often on our visit to Hong Kong. It's made with thin vermicelli rice noodles stir-fried with a mix of vegetables and curry powder. Eggs, shrimp and other protein are often added to make it a complete meal. It's extremely tasty with a flavorful kick of heat and makes great leftovers the next day!

YIELD: 4 SERVINGS

6 oz (170 g) dried fine vermicelli rice noodles (Wai Wai brand recommended if possible)

4 tbsp (60 ml) low sodium soy sauce

2 tsp (10 ml) fish sauce

2 tsp (10 g) Madras (hot) curry powder

1 tsp Chinese cooking wine or dry sherry

⅛ tsp ground white pepper

¼ tsp red pepper chili flakes

2 tsp (10 ml) cooking oil, divided

6 to 8 medium uncooked shrimp, shelled and deveined

2 garlic cloves, minced

½ tbsp (5 g) minced or grated fresh ginger

½ medium onion, very thinly sliced

1 medium red bell pepper, thinly sliced

1 cup (100 g) shredded Napa cabbage

½ medium carrot, julienned

2 eggs, beaten

Chopped fresh cilantro, for garnish (optional)

Green onions, thinly sliced on the bias, for garnish (optional)

Sesame seeds, for garnish (optional)

Start by soaking the dried vermicelli rice noodles in a large bowl covered in hot water for around 15 to 20 minutes or according to package directions. Drain and set aside. Cutting the noodles in half will help them submerge easier.

Meanwhile, in a small bowl, combine the soy sauce, fish sauce, curry powder, wine, white pepper and chili flakes for the sauce and set aside.

Heat 1 teaspoon of oil in a wok or large pan over medium heat. Add the shrimp and stir-fry until just cooked, about 1 to 2 minutes. Transfer to a plate and set aside.

Return the same pan back to the heat and add another teaspoon of oil. Sauté the garlic and ginger until fragrant, around 30 seconds. Next, add the onion, bell pepper, cabbage and carrots and allow to cook until tender, 3 to 4 minutes. Push the vegetables to one side and pour in the beaten eggs, scrambling until cooked. Add the vermicelli noodles and use tongs or chopsticks to separate and stir-fry until the noodles have softened, about 2 minutes.

Toss the shrimp back into the pan, give the sauce one quick stir and pour over the noodles. Gently toss until everything is combined, heated through and coated with sauce—about 1 to 2 minutes.

Serve hot with cilantro, green onions and sesame seeds, if desired.

SPICY PEANUT NOODLES

This is one of those really easy weeknight dinners that is delicious when served hot, warm or cold. It comes together in just one pot and it's surprisingly satisfying even without any meat. The creamy, nutty and savory sauce gets a little kick of heat from the Thai sweet chili sauce. What makes this even better is the flavors are awesome the next day too so you can make this the night before and take it along to the office, a potluck or even a barbecue!

YIELD: 4 SERVINGS

3½ cups (828 ml) chicken or vegetable broth

3 tbsp (83 g) peanut butter

2 tbsp (28 g) Thai sweet chili sauce (or 1 tbsp [15 ml] Sriracha)

2 tbsp (30 ml) low sodium soy sauce

½ tsp red pepper chili flakes

2 tsp (10 ml) cooking oil

3 garlic cloves, minced

½ tbsp (5 g) minced fresh ginger

1 small onion, diced

1 medium carrot, peeled, cut into thin matchsticks

1 red bell pepper, seeded, thinly sliced

8 oz (275 g) dried linguine or rice noodles

Fresh chopped cilantro, for garnish (optional)

2 green onions, thinly sliced, for garnish (optional)

Chopped roasted peanuts, for garnish (optional)

In a medium bowl, whisk together the broth, peanut butter, chili sauce, soy sauce and chili flakes until smooth and set aside.

Heat the cooking oil in a large heavy pot over medium-high heat. Add garlic and ginger and sauté until fragrant, around 30 seconds. Add the onion and cook until slightly softened, then add the carrot and red bell pepper. Continue to stir-fry until the vegetables are just starting to soften.

Add the sauce and noodles to the pot and bring to a boil while stirring. Reduce heat to a low simmer, give the pasta a good stir, cover with a lid and allow to cook for 10 to 12 minutes, stirring every 3 minutes.

Stir in water as needed, to taste, once pasta is al dente and liquid has evaporated, adjust seasonings and dish out.

Serve hot with cilantro, green onions or chopped peanuts, if desired.

TERIYAKI HONEY SHRIMP SOBA NOODLE BOWLS

This is a light and tasty dinner that comes together easily in just one pot. Buckwheat soba noodles are coated with a sweet and savory teriyaki sauce along with juicy shrimp and crisp-tender vegetables.

YIELD: 4 SERVINGS

• •

1¼ cup (296 ml) low sodium chicken broth

⅓ cup (79 ml) low sodium soy sauce

3 tbsp (42 g) honey

2 tbsp (30 ml) mirin

1½ tbsp (13 g) cornstarch

1 tsp rice wine vinegar

¼ cup (59 ml) fresh orange juice

1 garlic clove, finely minced

½ lb (225 g) shrimp, peeled and deveined

2 tsp (10 ml) cooking oil, divided

2 garlic cloves, minced

½ tbsp (5 g) fresh ginger, minced

6 oz (182 g) dried soba noodles

1 red bell pepper, thinly sliced

½ cup (25 g) matchstick carrots

⅓ cup (15 g) fresh chopped cilantro, divided (optional)

Sesame seeds, for garnish (optional)

In a medium bowl, whisk together the broth, soy sauce, honey, mirin, cornstarch, vinegar, orange juice and garlic for the sauce and set aside.

In a small bowl, add the shrimp and pour 1 tablespoon (15 ml) of sauce on top. Marinate for 15 minutes.

Heat 1 teaspoon of cooking oil in a large skillet over medium-high heat. Add shrimp and sear on both sides, until cooked and opaque, about 2 to 3 minutes. Transfer to a plate and set aside. Add another teaspoon of oil and sauté the garlic and ginger for 1 minute, until fragrant. Stir in the sauce and bring to a simmer for a minute or two until thickened. Add the soba noodles, bell pepper and carrots. Toss with tongs and cook until the noodles are softened, around 7 minutes. Adjust seasonings and add water as needed. Return the shrimp back to the pan and add half of the cilantro. Continue stir-frying until everything is combined and heated through and most of the liquid has been soaked up.

Divide into bowls, top with remaining cilantro and sesame seeds, if desired.

THAI PINEAPPLE CASHEW CHICKEN FRIED RICE

No matter how often I make fried rice, it's one of those dishes that never gets old. I love how easy it is to make and there are so many variations you can come up with. This Thai-inspired version is flavorful, delicious and one of my personal favorites. It has a fiery kick of heat from the curry and chili paste that gets balanced out by the sweet pineapples and crunchy cashews.

YIELD: 4 SERVINGS

1 tbsp (15 ml) low sodium soy sauce

2 tsp (10 ml) fish sauce

1 tsp mirin, Chinese rice wine or dry sherry

1 tsp red chili garlic paste

¼ tsp Madras curry powder

½ tsp cornstarch

½ tsp sugar

¼ tsp ground white pepper

Salt and black pepper to taste

1 medium chicken breast, cut into ½" (13-mm) chunks

5 tsp (25 ml) cooking oil, divided

3 garlic cloves, minced

¾ cup (115 g) frozen mixed vegetables

3 large eggs, lightly beaten

1½ cups (338 g) pineapple in ½" (13-mm) chunks

3 cups (585 g) day-old cooked rice, chilled with clumps separated

¼ cup (40 g) roasted unsalted cashews

Fresh chopped cilantro, for garnish (optional)

Sesame seeds, for garnish (optional)

In a small bowl, whisk together soy sauce, fish sauce, mirin, chili paste, curry powder, cornstarch, sugar, white pepper and salt and black pepper for the sauce.

Place the chicken in a medium bowl and spoon 1½ tablespoons (22 ml) of sauce over the top. Give it a good stir to combine.

Meanwhile, heat 2 teaspoons (10 ml) of oil in a wok or pan over high heat and sauté the garlic until fragrant, about 30 seconds. Add the chicken and stir-fry until almost browned and cooked through, about 5 to 6 minutes, then toss in the frozen mixed vegetables and cook for an additional 2 minutes. Push the ingredients to one side and pour in the beaten eggs. Scramble into small pieces until cooked and then transfer the entire contents of the pan to a large serving platter.

Return the pan to the heat and add 1 teaspoon of oil. Add the pineapple and sauté until slightly softened. Transfer to the same platter as the chicken and eggs. Return the pan back to the heat and add another 2 teaspoons (10 ml) of oil, spread the rice into the pan, breaking up any large chunks with a spatula and cook until the rice is slightly toasted. Add the platter of cooked meat and vegetables back into the pan and stir in the sauce. Adjust the seasonings then sprinkle in the cashews. Continue tossing and stirring well to combine everything until the rice is slightly toasted, about 3 minutes.

Serve hot with cilantro or sesame seeds, if desired.

Skip the Stove-top

My favorite thing about slow-cooker meals is the ability to throw everything into the pot and set-and-forget about it. However, some recipes (including mine) do call for some stove-top time which are necessary to help you achieve the full flavor or texture of the dish. I am all about quick and easy meals that are still equally delicious, so if there is a chance we can skip the stove-top then I am totally going to go for it!

This selection of recipes is perfect for when you want a truly fuss-free meal without having to sacrifice on flavor. Just toss and go—easy peasy!

ASIAN CHICKEN LETTUCE WRAPS

Lettuce wraps are a great choice for entertaining and make an easy family-style meal for busy weeknights. The kids get to join in the fun by making their own wraps and it's a sneaky and delicious way to get them (and my husband) to eat their veggies, which is always a bonus.

YIELD: 4 SERVINGS

1½ lb (683 g) boneless, skinless chicken thighs or breasts

⅓ cup (75 g) hoisin sauce, plus more for topping

2 tbsp (30 ml) low sodium soy sauce

1 tbsp (15 ml) rice vinegar

1 tsp sesame oil

½ tbsp (5 g) minced fresh ginger

2 shallots, finely chopped (or 1 medium onion)

2 garlic cloves, minced

½ tsp salt

¼ tsp black pepper

3 green onions, thinly sliced

2 celery stalks, finely chopped

1 red bell pepper, cored and finely chopped

1 head Boston or iceberg lettuce, leaves rinsed and patted dry

Shredded carrots, for garnish (optional)

Fresh chopped cilantro, for garnish (optional)

Sesame seeds, for garnish (optional)

Place the chicken in the bottom of the slow cooker. In a medium bowl, whisk together the hoisin sauce, soy sauce, vinegar, sesame oil, ginger, shallots, garlic, salt and pepper and pour over the chicken. Cook on low for 4 to 5 hours or on high for 2 to 3 hours. Remove the chicken from the slow cooker and shred with two forks. Return the shredded chicken back to the crock and stir in the green onions, celery and bell pepper. Turn the heat to high and cook for an additional 20 to 30 minutes or until the vegetables are slightly softened.

To assemble, scoop a spoonful of filling into the lettuce cups, then top with a few carrots, some cilantro, a sprinkle of sesame seeds and a drizzle of hoisin sauce, if desired.

BÁNH MÌ SANDWICHES

My parents used to buy Bánh Mì for us regularly at a Vietnamese deli downtown. They were freshly made on the spot with a choice of toppings and are still one of my favorite easy meals. If you've never tried Bánh Mì before, they are delectable Vietnamese sandwiches filled with an assortment of meat, pickled veggies and a creamy or buttery spread, layered on a crispy French baguette. They are incredibly tasty with a harmonious explosion of sweet, sour, spicy and savory flavors in every bite. The slow-cooked pork in this recipe is very versatile and you can use up any leftovers on nachos, tacos or over a bed of rice.

YIELD: 6 SERVINGS

½ cup (118 ml) vinegar

1½ tbsp (18 g) sugar

1 tsp salt

1 medium carrot, peeled and cut into matchsticks

1 medium daikon, peeled and cut into matchsticks

1 cup (237 ml) water

⅓ cup (79 ml) low sodium soy sauce

2½ tbsp (38 ml) fish sauce

1 tbsp (16 g) hoisin sauce

½ cup (100 g) brown sugar

2 tsp (10 g) red chili garlic paste

1 tsp rice vinegar

½ tsp minced fresh ginger

5 garlic cloves, minced

2 stalks lemongrass, trimmed and sliced thinly

1 medium onion, roughly chopped

2 lb (910 g) pork shoulder or butt, fat trimmed

1 tbsp (15 ml) fresh lime juice

2 long baguettes cut in thirds or 4–6 small rolls, split lengthwise

Whipped or softened unsalted butter

Pâté (optional)

1 English cucumber, thinly sliced

Jalapeños, thinly sliced

1 cup (50 g) chopped fresh cilantro leaves

Sriracha sauce (optional)

In a medium sealable bowl or a mason jar, combine the vinegar, sugar and salt and then add the carrots and daikon. Seal it all up and store in the refrigerator until ready to assemble the sandwiches.

In the bottom of a slow cooker, combine the water, soy sauce, fish sauce, hoisin sauce, brown sugar, chili paste and rice vinegar. Toss in the ginger, garlic, lemongrass and onion. Nestle the pork in the middle and coat with the liquid. Cook on low for 7 to 8 hours or on high for 4 to 5 hours, rotating once during the cooking process and coating with some sauce.

Transfer the pork to a cutting board and shred using two forks. Dump the pork back into the slow cooker, squeeze in some lime juice and toss to combine with the remaining sauce.

Slice the baguettes or rolls in half lengthwise. Spread a thin layer of butter on the bottom half of each roll along with some pâté, if desired. Top with a spoonful of pork, some pickled vegetables, cucumber slices, a jalapeño slice and some fresh cilantro pieces. Drizzle with Sriracha sauce, if desired. Serve immediately.

HOISIN CHILI CHICKEN TACOS

Taco Tuesdays are one of our favorite nights and I love changing up the flavors to keep things interesting. These tacos are filled with tender juicy chicken coated in a sweet and smoky Asian-inspired sauce. They make an easy weeknight meal and the kids get to have fun assembling their own plate.

YIELD: 4 SERVINGS

1½ lb (455 g) boneless, skinless chicken thighs or chicken breasts

½ cup (115 g) hoisin sauce

¼ cup (55 g) sweet chili sauce

2 tbsp (30 ml) low sodium soy sauce

2 tsp (3 g) fresh ginger, grated

3 garlic cloves, minced

½ cup (50 g) shredded Napa cabbage

½ cup (50 g) shredded red cabbage

¼ cup (15 g) thinly shredded carrots

2 tbsp (30 ml) rice vinegar

½ tsp sugar

Corn or flour tortillas, toasted if desired

Fresh chopped cilantro, for garnish

Place the chicken in the bottom of the slow cooker. In a medium bowl, combine the hoisin sauce, sweet chili sauce, soy sauce, ginger and garlic. Pour over the chicken and cover with the lid. Cook on low for 3 to 4 hours. Transfer the chicken to a cutting board and shred using two forks.

While the chicken is cooking, toss together the Napa and red cabbage, carrots, vinegar and sugar in a large bowl. Cover and store in the fridge until ready to use.

Assemble the tacos by filling each tortilla with some chicken and a layer of slaw. Garnish with a sprinkle of fresh cilantro.

NOTE: Use already shredded cabbage slaw for convenience, if desired.

HONEY GARLIC CHICKEN SLIDERS

Sliders are a terrific addition to your game-day menu and also a fun and tasty way to change up your weeknight dinner. The sweet and sticky honey garlic chicken cooks up tender and makes a delicious filling alongside the crunchy cabbage slaw.

YIELD: 4–6 SERVINGS

1½ lb (683 g) skinless, bone-in chicken thighs or chicken breasts

¼ cup (59 ml) low sodium soy sauce

3 tbsp (48 g) hoisin sauce

3 tbsp (48 g) Thai sweet chili sauce

2 tbsp (30 ml) balsamic glaze

2 tbsp (42 g) honey

3 garlic cloves, minced

1 medium onion, diced

½ cup (50 g) shredded Napa cabbage

½ cup (50 g) shredded red cabbage

¼ cup (15 g) thinly shredded carrots

2 tbsp (30 ml) rice vinegar

½ tsp sugar

Slider buns

Fresh cilantro, for garnish

Sriracha (optional)

Sesame seeds, for garnish (optional)

Place the chicken directly into the bottom of the slow cooker. Combine the soy sauce, hoisin sauce, chili sauce, balsamic glaze, honey, garlic and onion, and pour evenly over the chicken. Cook on low for 4 to 5 hours. Transfer the chicken to a cutting board and shred into thin strips with two forks.

While the chicken is cooking, combine the Napa cabbage, red cabbage, carrots, rice vinegar and sugar in a large bowl. Cover and store in the fridge until ready to use.

Divide the shredded chicken evenly among the slider buns. Layer with some slaw, cilantro and add a drizzle of Sriracha and sesame seeds, if desired.

MANGO ASIAN TURKEY WRAPS

These tropical Asian-inspired wraps are made with tender spiced turkey strips covered in a sweet and tangy mango sauce. The sunny flavors make these a tasty and refreshing meal during the warmer summer months.

YIELD: 4 SERVINGS

1½ lb (683 g) boneless, skinless turkey thighs or turkey breasts

2½ cups (300 g) sweet frozen or fresh mango, cubed

⅓ cup (79 ml) low sodium soy sauce

3 tbsp (63 g) honey

½ tbsp (7 ml) sesame oil

2 tsp (10 ml) rice vinegar

2 garlic cloves, minced

½ tsp minced fresh ginger

Salt and black pepper, to taste

Flour tortillas

3 lettuce leaves, torn in half

1 red bell pepper, thinly sliced

½ cup (38 g) shredded carrots

1 green onion, thinly sliced

½ cup (60 g) roasted cashews, chopped

Chopped fresh cilantro

Place the turkey in the bottom of the slow cooker. In a blender, add mango, soy sauce, honey, sesame oil, vinegar, garlic and ginger and purée until smooth. Pour over the turkey and cover with the lid. Cook on low for 5 to 6 hours or on high for 3 to 4 hours. Remove the turkey and shred with two forks. Return to the slow cooker and coat with the sauce. Season with salt and pepper to taste.

Spread a spoonful of sauce on each tortilla. Layer with the lettuce and turkey mixture followed by bell pepper, carrot, green onion, chopped cashews and fresh cilantro. Roll up the tortilla and top with extra sauce, if desired.

PANANG CURRY WITH ROTI

I am a sucker for all types of curries, which is completely the opposite of when I was younger.
I had a taste of Panang curry for the first time on my initial visit to Thailand with my parents and it was the
most delicious curry I had ever had. It was richer, sweeter and creamier than most Thai curries and just as
comforting and satisfying. Serve it over a bed of rice or a piece of warm Roti or Naan for a hearty meal.

YIELD: 4 SERVINGS

1 lb (454 g) skinless chicken thighs

1 medium sweet potato, peeled, cut into 1″ (2.5-cm) cubes

1 medium onion, diced

½ cup (100 g) diced tomato

3 garlic cloves, minced

1 tsp minced fresh ginger

1 cup (237 ml) low sodium chicken broth

3 tbsp (48 g) Panang curry paste

½ cup (115 g) tomato paste

3 tbsp (45 ml) Thai fish sauce

3 tbsp (38 g) brown sugar

4 kaffir leaves, stems discarded, finely chopped OR zest & juice of 1 lime

¼–½ tsp crushed red pepper flakes, to taste

1 (14-oz [385-ml]) can coconut milk

Toasted Roti or Naan bread, for serving

Fresh chopped cilantro, for garnish

Add the chicken, sweet potato, onion, tomato, garlic and ginger to the bottom of a 4- to 5-quart (3.8- to 4.7-L) slow cooker.

In a small bowl, combine the broth, curry paste, tomato paste, fish sauce, brown sugar, kaffir leaves and pepper flakes. Pour the mixture over the chicken. Cook on low for 6 to 8 hours or high for 3 to 4 hours. Remove the lid and stir in the coconut milk. Cook on high for an additional 20 minutes or until heated through.

Serve with a few pieces of some toasted Roti or Naan bread and garnish with some cilantro, if desired.

NOTE: If you can't find Panang curry paste, substitute by mixing: 2½ tablespoons (38 g) red curry paste, ½ teaspoon cumin and ½ teaspoon coriander.

SRIRACHA HONEY PULLED PORK SLIDERS

Both of my parents were spice fiends so there was always a bottle of Sriracha in our fridge for as long as I could remember. We now have that same red bottle in our fridge and we add it to almost everything including these tasty sliders. The sweet and spicy combo makes them irresistible at parties yet still easy enough for busy weeknights.

YIELD: 4 SERVINGS

2 lb (910 g) pork roast, trimmed of excess fat

1 tsp sea salt

1 tsp black pepper

1 medium onion, finely diced

4 garlic cloves, minced

½ cup (118 ml) low sodium soy sauce

⅓ cup (75 g) tomato paste

¼ cup (50 g) dark brown sugar

¼ cup (60 ml) Sriracha

3 tbsp (63 g) honey

3 tbsp (45 ml) rice wine vinegar or apple cider vinegar

Slider rolls, split, toasted

Pickled coleslaw, for topping

Place the roast in the bottom of the slow cooker and season with salt and pepper. Combine the onion, garlic, soy sauce, tomato paste, sugar, Sriracha, honey and vinegar in a small bowl and rub well into the roast. Cook on low for 6 to 7 hours.

Transfer the pork to a cutting board and shred into pieces with two forks.

Serve over slider rolls, with some extra sauce and top with coleslaw.

SUMMER ROLLS WITH GLAZED BROWN SUGAR PORK

I spent many Saturday mornings helping my mom assemble and wrap summer rolls when I was younger.
We had an efficient setup where I would get the rice paper sheets ready and have them lined
up along with the plates of fresh cut vegetables and assortment of meat or shrimp.
They are great for potlucks and barbecues and make a light and healthy snack.

YIELD: 6–8 SERVINGS

½ cup (110 g) hoisin sauce

½ cup (118 ml) low sodium soy sauce

3 tbsp (38 g) brown sugar

3 tbsp (45 ml) fish sauce

½ tbsp (8 g) red chili garlic paste

3 garlic cloves, minced

1 medium onion, peeled and sliced

⅔ lb (302 g) boneless pork shoulder roast

3 tbsp (45 g) peanut butter

2 tbsp (30 ml) rice vinegar

2 tbsp (30 ml) soy sauce

2 tsp (10 g) honey

½–1 tsp of red pepper chili flakes

1–2 tbsp (15–30 ml) water

1 package (6 or 8 inch [15 or 20 cm]) round rice paper sheets

8–10 green lettuce leaves, washed, dried and torn

1 cup (180 g) cooked rice vermicelli, rinsed and drained

1 large cucumber, cut into thin strips

1 large carrot, peeled, cut into thin strips

⅓ cup (26 g) fresh cilantro

In the bottom of a 5- to 6-quart (4.7- to 5.7-L) slow cooker, combine the hoisin sauce, soy sauce, brown sugar, fish sauce, chili paste, garlic and onion. Place the pork roast in the middle and spoon the liquid over. Cook on low for 7 to 8 hours, until the pork is very tender, rotating once during the cooking process, if possible. When the pork is ready, shred the meat with two forks into thin strips and combine with the remaining sauce.

In a medium bowl, combine the peanut butter, vinegar, soy sauce, honey, chili flakes and water for the dipping sauce. Taste and adjust seasoning and add more water, if necessary to thin out. Cover and store in the fridge until ready to serve.

Add hot water to a large bowl, cake or pie pan. Working with one rice wrapper at a time, quickly dip each wrapper in hot water for about 2 to 3 seconds and lay it on a flat plastic cutting board or plate. The wrapper will soften up as it sits for a few seconds.

Lay a piece of lettuce on the bottom third of the softened wrapper. Add a bit of the noodles, cucumber, carrot, cilantro and pork, being careful not to overfill.

Fold up the bottom edge over the filling, then fold in the sides towards the center. Roll up tightly using your hands to tuck-and-roll the filling as you are rolling up. Repeat with the remaining ingredients.

Place on a plate and serve with the peanut dipping sauce.

VIETNAMESE LEMONGRASS PORK CHOPS WITH RICE

This recipe involves tender pork chops slow cooked in a sweet and savory marinade with refreshing undertones of lemongrass. These were classic Vietnamese flavors my mom used a lot when she was preparing richer cuts of meat. The savory flavors go beautifully with some rice and pickled vegetables on the side.

YIELD: 4 SERVINGS

4 large pork chops

½ tsp salt

½ tsp black pepper

2 tsp (10 ml) cooking oil

1 large onion, thinly sliced

2 garlic cloves, peeled and smashed

1 green onion, roughly chopped

1 lemongrass stalk, outer layer removed

1 (1" [2.5-cm]) piece fresh ginger root, peeled

¼ cup (59 ml) fish sauce

3 tbsp (38 g) brown sugar

2 tbsp (28 g) hoisin sauce

½ tsp red garlic chili paste, to taste

Zest of 1 lime

½ cup (118 ml) vinegar

1½ tbsp (18 g) sugar

1 tsp salt

1 medium carrot, peeled and cut into matchsticks

1 medium daikon, peeled and cut into matchsticks

Cooked rice, for serving

1 green onion, thinly sliced, for garnish (optional)

Chopped fresh cilantro, for garnish (optional)

Sesame seeds, for garnish (optional)

Season the pork chops with salt and pepper. Heat the oil in a skillet over medium-high heat, add the pork then the onion and cook until brown, about 2 minutes on both sides. Dump the contents into the bottom of your slow cooker.

Combine garlic, green onion, lemongrass, ginger, fish sauce, brown sugar, hoisin sauce, chili paste and lime zest in a blender and blend until smooth. Pour into the slow cooker, covering the pork chops. Cook on high for 2 to 3 hours or on low for 5 to 6 hours.

In a medium sealable bowl or a mason jar, combine the vinegar, sugar and salt. Then add the carrot and daikon. Seal the bowl or jar and store in the refrigerator until ready to serve.

Serve with cooked rice and add the pickled vegetables on the side. Garnish with green onions, cilantro and sesame seeds, if desired.

Fiery Favorites

When I was younger, I was the only one in my family who could not handle a touch of heat. Anytime my mom made anything spicy, she would scoop out a small portion just for me prior to adding in any hot sauce or chili peppers. As I got older, my spice tolerance increased and now I love anything hot.

If you are a fellow heat-seeker, turn up the heat with the fiery recipes in this chapter. Depending on your comfort level, they range from just a warm tingle to setting your mouth on fire. As always, feel free to tone down the amounts according to your taste and have that glass of water handy!

SZECHUAN BEEF

My husband and I are big fans of Szechuan cuisine since most of their dishes are spicy, hot and bold in flavor. This dish is a popular menu item made with tender beef strips and crunchy vegetables covered in a fiery and flavorful peppercorn sauce. Heat seekers, this one's for you!

YIELD: 4 SERVINGS

¼ cup plus 1½ tbsp (43 g) cornstarch, divided

¼ tsp black pepper

2 lb (910 g) flank steak, cut across the grain into thin strips

2 tsp (10 ml) cooking oil

½ cup (118 ml) low sodium chicken broth

2 tbsp (28 g) red chili garlic paste

2 tbsp (30 ml) soy sauce

1 tbsp (15 ml) balsamic vinegar

1 tbsp (15 ml) Chinese rice wine or dry sherry

1 tbsp (14 g) spicy fermented bean curd

2 tsp (10 ml) dark soy sauce (leave out if you can't find this)

3 garlic cloves, minced

½ tsp fresh ginger, minced

½ tbsp (7 g) Sichuan peppercorns OR ½ tsp red pepper chili flakes, to taste

2 tbsp (30 ml) cool water

6–8 dried whole red chili peppers

1 leek, thinly sliced

1 red bell pepper, thinly sliced

Cooked rice, for serving

Sesame seeds, for garnish (optional)

In a large zip-top bag, toss together ¼ cup (30 g) cornstarch and black pepper. Add the beef to the bag and give it a little shake until well coated.

In a large skillet, heat the oil over medium-high heat. Sear the beef for about 1 to 2 minutes on both sides and add to the slow cooker.

In a medium bowl, whisk together the chicken broth, chili garlic paste, soy sauce, vinegar, wine, fermented bean curd, dark soy sauce, garlic, ginger and peppercorns until dissolved, then pour over the beef. Cook on low for about 3 to 4 hours.

About 30 minutes prior to serving, whisk together the remaining cornstarch with the water in a small bowl and stir into the slow cooker. Stir in the chili peppers, leeks and red bell pepper and cover with the lid. Turn the heat to high and allow the sauce to cook and thicken up for about 20 to 30 minutes.

Serve over rice and garnish with sesame seeds, if desired.

BÁNH MÌ QUINOA BOWLS

I love that food served in bowls is showing up everywhere these days. We grew up with a variety of rice bowls in our house, but there are days I love swapping out the rice for quinoa. This version is an adaptation on Bánh Mì, our favorite Vietnamese sandwich. The pork is slow cooked in a sweet and spicy sauce infused with lemongrass, and served with crunchy pickled vegetables and fresh herbs. The refreshing flavors get a punch of heat from the drizzle of Sriracha, creating excitement in every bite!

YIELD: 4-6 SERVINGS

½ cup (118 ml) vinegar

1½ tbsp (18 g) sugar

1 tsp salt

1 medium carrot, peeled and cut into matchsticks

1 medium daikon, peeled and cut into matchsticks

1 cup (237 ml) chicken broth

⅓ cup (80 ml) low sodium soy sauce

2½ tbsp (38 ml) fish sauce

1 tbsp (16 g) hoisin sauce

½ cup (100 g) brown sugar

2 tsp (10 g) red chili garlic paste

1 tsp rice vinegar

½ tsp minced fresh ginger

5 garlic cloves, minced

2 stalks lemongrass, trimmed and thinly sliced

1 medium onion, roughly chopped

2 lb (910 g) pork shoulder or butt, fat trimmed

1 tbsp (15 ml) fresh lime juice

Cooked quinoa

1 cucumber, thinly sliced

Chopped fresh cilantro, for garnish

Chopped fresh mint, for garnish (optional)

Sliced jalapeños, for garnish (optional)

Sriracha, for serving (optional)

In a medium sealable bowl or a mason jar, combine the vinegar, sugar and salt together and then add the carrot and daikon. Give it a seal then store in the refrigerator until ready to assemble the bowls.

In the bottom of the slow cooker, combine the broth, soy sauce, fish sauce, hoisin sauce, brown sugar, chili paste and rice vinegar. Toss in the ginger, garlic, lemongrass and onion—place the pork in the middle and coat with some liquid. Cook on low for 5 to 6 hours.

Transfer the pork to a cutting board and shred using two forks. Dump it back into the slow cooker then add the lime juice and toss to coat evenly.

Divide the quinoa into bowls and layer with some pork, pickled vegetables, cucumber slices and cilantro. Top with mint, sliced jalapeños and a drizzle of Sriracha, if desired.

NOTE: Substitute quinoa with cooked brown rice or grain of your choice if desired.

CHILI HOISIN GLAZED STICKY MEATBALLS

Meatballs make a fun and easy appetizer and can easily be turned into a meal by serving them on a bed of rice with a side of vegetables. Each meatball is coated in a sticky, savory sauce made with chili paste, hoisin, fresh ginger and a touch of honey. I put them under the broiler for a few minutes to retain their shape before transferring them to the slow cooker. This allows the flavors to meld together while cooking up nice and tender.

YIELD: 6 SERVINGS

1 lb (455 g) ground beef

1 lb (455 g) ground pork

2 large eggs

¾ cup (70 g) panko breadcrumbs

4 minced garlic cloves, divided

1 medium onion, finely chopped

2 green onions, thinly sliced (reserve 2 tsp [2 g] for garnish)

Salt and pepper to taste

⅓ cup (75 g) hoisin sauce

¼ cup (59 ml) low sodium soy sauce

1 tbsp (16 g) red chili garlic paste

1 tbsp (21 g) honey

1 tsp sesame oil

¼ tsp red pepper chili flakes, or to taste

½ tsp ground ginger

Sesame seeds, for garnish (optional)

Line two large baking sheets with parchment paper or foil sprayed with non-stick cooking spray and set aside.

In a large bowl, combine the beef, pork, eggs, breadcrumbs, half the garlic, onion, green onions and salt and pepper. Using your hands, mix and form into 1- to 1½-inch (2.5-to 4-cm) diameter balls, then place onto the prepared baking sheets in a single layer. Broil in batches on high for 5 to 6 minutes, flipping halfway through, or until just browned (meat will not be cooked through).

Meanwhile, whisk together the hoisin sauce, soy sauce, chili paste, honey, sesame oil, chili flakes, remaining garlic and ginger. Transfer the browned meatballs to the bottom of the slow cooker and pour the sauce mixture over them, coating well.

Cook on low for 5 to 6 hours or on high for 2 to 3 hours. Stir gently every 30 minutes to coat evenly and ensure that the meatballs do not stick.

Serve with sliced green onions and sesame seeds for garnish, if desired.

DAN DAN NOODLES

Dan Dan Noodles is a classic Chinese Sichuan dish with a rich and spicy meat sauce served over soft egg noodles. For this version, I left out the preserved vegetables and scaled down the spice level slightly. If you are a spice fiend, feel free to up the chili oil.

YIELD: 2–3 SERVINGS

¼ cup (59 ml) water

3 tbsp (45 ml) dark soy sauce

2 tbsp (32 g) chili oil or red chili garlic paste, to taste

1 tbsp (15 ml) Chinese black rice vinegar or balsamic vinegar

1 tbsp (15 ml) Chinese rice wine or dry sherry

1 tbsp (15 g) tahini or peanut butter

2 tsp (10 ml) sesame oil

1 tsp sugar

½ tsp ground Sichuan pepper

¼ tsp red pepper chili flakes, to taste

¼ tsp five-spice powder

2 tsp (10 ml) cooking oil

½ lb (225 g) ground pork

2 garlic cloves, minced

1 tsp minced fresh ginger

½ lb (228 g) fresh or dried egg noodles, rice noodles or spaghetti noodles

2 green onions, thinly sliced, for garnish (optional)

¼ cup (30 g) dry-roasted peanuts, chopped, for garnish (optional)

In a medium bowl, whisk together the water, soy sauce, chili oil, vinegar, wine, tahini, sesame oil, sugar, Sichuan pepper, chili flakes and five-spice powder until combined and set aside.

Heat the oil in a skillet over medium heat, add the pork and cook until brown, about 6 to 8 minutes, crumbling into small pieces. Add the garlic and ginger and cook until fragrant, about 1 to 2 minutes. Dump everything into the slow cooker and pour the sauce over the top. Cook on low for 3 to 4 hours or on high for 1 to 2 hours.

Meanwhile, prepare the noodles according to package instructions, then drain and divide into separate bowls. Layer with the meat mixture and top with additional sauce. Sprinkle with green onions and peanuts, if desired.

FIRECRACKER CHICKEN NACHOS

We love spicy foods at our house and when you add nachos to the mix, it's sure to be a hit with my family. This firecracker chicken is sweet, fiery and sticky delicious! It's similar to the popular Sweet and Sour Chicken but packs a punch from the buffalo sauce and can be easily adapted for those that are spice-sensitive. Serve them layered over crunchy tortilla chips and pickled vegetables and you've got one amazing appetizer or game-day snack!

YIELD: 4 SERVINGS

½ cup (118 ml) vinegar

1½ tbsp (18 g) sugar

1 tsp salt

¼ cup (10 g) shredded carrots

½ cup (50 g) shredded red cabbage

½ cup (50 g) shredded Napa cabbage

¾ cup (177 ml) buffalo sauce

⅓ cup (75 g) Thai sweet chili sauce

3 tbsp (63 g) honey

1 tbsp (15 ml) soy sauce

¼ tsp red pepper chili flakes, to taste

1½ lb (683 g) boneless, skinless chicken thighs or breasts

1 (13-oz [368-g]) bag restaurant-style tortilla chips

1 cup (113 g) shredded Monterey Jack cheese

1 cup (113 g) shredded Sharp Cheddar cheese

¼ cup (17 g) sliced pickled jalapeños

1 green onion, sliced thinly

½ cup (20 g) fresh cilantro leaves

Lime wedges, for serving

Preheat your oven to 425°F (218°C).

In a medium sealable bowl, combine the vinegar, sugar and salt then add the carrots, the red and Napa cabbage. Cover the bowl and store in the refrigerator until ready to assemble the nachos.

Combine the buffalo sauce, sweet chili sauce, honey, soy sauce and chili flakes in the bottom of the slow cooker. Nestle the chicken in the middle, then coat with some liquid. Cook on low for 3 to 4 hours. Transfer to a cutting board and shred with two forks.

Line a large baking sheet with foil or parchment paper. Arrange half of the chips on the prepared sheet and top with half of the shredded chicken, then layer with half of each cheese. Top with another layer of chips and repeat the toppings.

Broil or bake in the oven until the cheese is melted and bubbling, about 5 minutes. Remove the tray from the oven and top with jalapeños, green onions and fresh cilantro.

Drizzle with the remaining marinade sauce from the pork. Serve immediately with lime wedges, if desired.

KIMCHI CHICKEN AND RICE

When I was pregnant with my son I had a constant craving for kimchi, which motivated me to learn how to make my own. It's a traditional Korean side dish of fermented vegetables that adds flavor to soups, stews and fried rice. This is an adaptation of kimchi fried rice and is one of our favorite dishes to use up aged kimchi. We add ground chicken and instead of pan frying the rice, we toss it into the slow cooker for the flavors to meld, making this an easy weeknight meal.

YIELD: 4 SERVINGS

2 tsp (9 g) sesame oil

½ lb (225 g) ground chicken

1 cup (100 g) over-fermented (aged) kimchi, chopped into small pieces

2 garlic cloves, minced

2½ cups (420 g) day-old cooked rice

¼ cup (60 ml) kimchi juice

2 tbsp (30 ml) low sodium soy sauce

1 tbsp (15 g) Gochujang (or to taste)

¼ tsp black pepper

Fried egg, for serving (optional)

1 green onion, thinly sliced, for garnish (optional)

1 sheet of roasted seaweed, cut into thin strips for serving (optional)

Sesame seeds, for garnish (optional)

Heat the sesame oil in a large non-stick skillet or wok on medium-high heat. Add the ground chicken and cook until lightly browned, crumbling as it cooks, about 4 to 5 minutes. Add the kimchi and garlic and stir-fry for another 2 minutes. Transfer everything into a slow cooker. Stir in the rice, kimchi juice, soy sauce, Gochujang and black pepper.

Cook on low for 2 to 3 hours or high for 1 to 1½ hours. Stir and adjust seasonings.

Serve in bowls and top with a fried egg, green onions, roasted seaweed and sesame seeds, if desired.

MAPO TOFU

Mapo Tofu was always a favorite at our house. It's a classic Sichuan dish typically made with silken tofu and ground pork coated in a fiery chili-paste sauce. I used firm tofu for this version since it holds up better in the slow cooker but still tastes just as delicious. You can also adjust the amount of chilies to make this as mild or spicy as you like. We like serving this with a bowl of rice to soak up all that flavorful sauce.

YIELD: 4 SERVINGS

1 cup (237 ml) chicken broth

2 tbsp (30 ml) low sodium soy sauce

2 tbsp (30 ml) rice wine vinegar

1 tsp fermented black beans (rinsed) or paste (optional)

½ tsp ground Sichuan pepper OR red pepper chili flakes, to taste

1 tsp sesame oil

2 green onions, thinly sliced, divided

1 (14-oz [400-g]) package firm tofu, pressed, drained and cut into ½" (1.2-cm) cubes

3 tsp (15 ml) cooking oil

1 lb (455 g) lean ground pork

4 garlic cloves, minced

1 tsp minced fresh ginger

2 tbsp (32 g) chili bean paste

2-3 fresh or dried red chilies, roughly chopped

2 tbsp (16 g) cornstarch

2 tbsp (30 ml) cold water

Cooked rice, for serving

Sesame seeds, for garnish (optional)

To make the sauce, in a medium bowl, whisk together the broth, soy sauce, vinegar, fermented black beans, Sichuan pepper, sesame oil and half of the green onions until combined.

Add the cubed tofu to the bottom of the slow cooker. Heat the oil in a skillet over medium-high heat, crumble the pork with a spatula and cook until brown, 4 to 5 minutes. Add garlic, ginger, chili bean paste and dried red chilies and cook until fragrant, 1 to 2 minutes. Stir in the sauce and bring to a quick boil. Remove from the heat and pour the mixture into the slow cooker, covering the tofu. Cook on low for 5 to 6 hours or on high for 2 to 3 hours. Stir in the remaining green onions and allow to cook for an additional 10 minutes on high.

To thicken the sauce, whisk together the cornstarch and water in a small bowl and stir into the slow cooker and allow to cook and thicken up for 20 to 30 minutes.

Serve with rice and sprinkle with sesame seeds, if desired.

NOTE: To press the tofu, remove the tofu from the packaging and drain the water. Place the block between paper towels or a kitchen towel. Wrap firmly around the block and transfer to a plate. Top with another plate and place a heavy object (book, cans) on top of the plate. Allow tofu to press for 30 minutes to an hour. Drain and cut into small cubes.

MANCHURIAN CHICKEN

My husband and I used to frequent this Hakka restaurant that served the most delicious Indo-Chinese food. It was a small family-owned restaurant and one of our favorite dishes was their Manchurian Chicken. It's made with crispy bite-sized chicken covered in a rich, spicy and savory gravy that is simply extraordinary over a bowl of plain rice.

YIELD: 4 SERVINGS

1 cup plus 1½ tbsp (138 g) cornstarch, divided

½ tsp black pepper

1½ lb (683 g) boneless, skinless chicken thighs or breasts, cut into bite-sized cubes

2 tsp (10 ml) cooking oil

1 cup (237 ml) low sodium chicken broth

½ cup (118 ml) soy sauce

¼ cup (55 g) red chili garlic paste

¼ cup (55 g) tomato paste or ketchup

2 tbsp (30 ml) apple cider vinegar

½ tsp red pepper chili flakes, to taste

4 garlic cloves, finely minced

½ tbsp (5 g) minced fresh ginger

1 medium onion, diced

2 tbsp (30 ml) cool water

2 bell peppers, diced (1 red, 1 green for color)

Cooked rice, for serving

1 green onion, thinly sliced, for garnish (optional)

In a large zip-top bag, toss together 1 cup (125 g) cornstarch and black pepper. Next add the chicken to the bag, and give it a little shake until well coated.

In a large skillet, heat the oil over medium-high heat. Add the chicken and cook for about 1 to 2 minutes on both sides, then add it to the bottom of the slow cooker. In a medium bowl, whisk the broth, soy sauce, chili paste, tomato paste, vinegar, chili flakes, garlic, ginger and onion and pour over the chicken. Cook on low for about 3 to 4 hours.

About 30 minutes prior to serving, whisk together the remaining cornstarch with water in a small bowl and stir into the slow cooker along with the bell peppers. Turn the heat to high and allow the sauce to cook and thicken up for about 20 to 30 minutes and the bell peppers to become tender-crisp.

Serve hot over rice. Garnish with green onions, if desired.

SPICY CHAR SIU CHICKEN THIGHS

This dish is a twist on the popular Chinese BBQ pork typically found in Cantonese restaurants. Tender chicken thighs get smothered in a sweet, smoky hoisin sauce along with a touch of spicy Sriracha. I like to finish them briefly under the broiler for a crispy coating which also helps to seal in the flavor.

YIELD: 4 SERVINGS

8 bone-in chicken thighs

3 tbsp (48 g) hoisin sauce

2 tbsp (42 g) honey

2 tbsp (30 ml) low sodium soy sauce

2 tbsp (30 ml) Sriracha

1 tbsp (32 ml) Chinese rice wine or dry sherry

1 tsp fresh grated ginger

2 garlic cloves, minced

½ tsp five-spice powder

1 green onion, thinly sliced, for garnish (optional)

Sesame seeds, for garnish (optional)

Place the chicken inside the bottom of the slow cooker.

In a medium bowl, combine the hoisin sauce, honey, soy sauce, Sriracha, wine, ginger, garlic and five-spice. Pour over the chicken, coating well. Cook on low for 3 to 4 hours.

Gently transfer the thighs to a wire-rack on a foil-lined baking sheet. Brush with the remaining sauce and broil for 5 minutes or until caramelized.

Remove from the oven and garnish with green onions and sesame seeds, if desired.

THAI GREEN CURRY BEEF WITH ZUCCHINI NOODLES

There's something about curry that just screams comfort food to me. My mom used to make a big ole pot for us regularly and we always looked forward to having the flavor-packed leftovers for lunch the next day. Green curry adds a wonderfully exotic and vivid aroma and instantly heightens the flavors of any simple dish. I served this over zucchini noodles to lighten the dish up but it goes wonderfully with a bowl of steaming hot rice too.

YIELD: 4 SERVINGS

2 cups (474 ml) low sodium chicken broth

3 tbsp (48 g) green curry paste

3 tbsp (45 ml) fish sauce

1 tbsp (12 g) brown sugar

2 tsp (10 g) red chili garlic paste, to taste

4 garlic cloves, minced

2 tbsp (16 g) minced fresh ginger

2 tsp (10 ml) cooking oil

1½ lb (683 g) beef chuck roast, trimmed of fat and sliced into rounds

3 shallots, diced

2 large carrots, peeled and cut into 1" (2.5-cm) rounds

3 cups (710 ml) full fat canned coconut milk

½ cup (165 g) cauliflower florets

1 red bell pepper, cut into 1" (2.5-cm) chunks

1 tbsp (15 ml) lime juice plus more for seasoning

Zucchini noodles (spiralized zucchini) or cooked rice, for serving

3 tbsp (15 g) chopped fresh cilantro

In a medium bowl, whisk the broth, curry paste, fish sauce, brown sugar, chili paste, garlic and ginger until combined; set aside.

Heat the oil in a skillet over medium-high heat. Add the beef and sear for 2 to 3 minutes on one side. After you flip the meat, toss in the shallots and cook the meat for 2 to 3 minutes. Then transfer entire contents to the slow cooker. Toss in the carrots then pour the sauce over top. Cook on low for 5 to 7 hours. About 30 minutes before serving, stir in the coconut milk, cauliflower, bell peppers and lime juice and cook on high for an additional 30 minutes or until vegetables are crisp. Taste and adjust seasonings as needed. Remove the beef and shred with two forks or cut into bite-sized pieces.

Serve hot with the vegetables and sauce over spiralized zucchini noodles or cooked rice. Sprinkle with cilantro and more lime juice, if desired.

NOTE: Zucchini noodles can be cooked by stirring them into the slow cooker along with the coconut milk and cooking for 20 to 30 minutes.

Meatless Mondays

When we were growing up, my mom always made sure that there were a few vegetable dishes alongside our meals. She loved her veggies and taught us at a very young age to embrace bok choy, broccoli, eggplant, water spinach and anything else she could grow in her garden.

Whether you're trying to incorporate more plant-based foods into your diet or looking for new ideas, these meatless dishes are sure to keep your taste buds happy and your tummies full. They are infused with aromatic herbs and bold spices that you'll welcome with open arms and might even make you want to skip over that Kung Pao Chicken.

GENERAL TSO'S BRUSSELS SPROUTS AND SWEET POTATOES

This favorite takeout dish gets a meatless makeover using one of my favorite side dish duos—Brussels sprouts and sweet potatoes. They are coated in the popular spicy, sweet and tangy General Tso's sauce that we love, and are a fun twist to get your family excited about their veggies. Serve it alongside your favorite protein or enjoy it on a bed of quinoa or rice.

YIELD: 4–5 SERVINGS

1 lb (453 g) Brussels sprouts, trimmed and halved

1 lb (453 g) sweet potatoes, peeled, and cut into bite-sized 1" (2.5-cm) chunks

1 tbsp (15 ml) olive oil

¼–½ tsp sea salt, to taste

⅓ cup (79 ml) low sodium soy sauce

1 tbsp (16 g) hoisin sauce

2 tbsp (30 ml) balsamic vinegar

2 tbsp (42 g) honey

1 tbsp (16 g) ketchup or tomato paste

½ tsp sesame oil

3 garlic cloves, minced

1 tsp fresh ginger, minced

2 tsp (6 g) cornstarch

1–2 tsp (6–11 g) red chili garlic paste, to taste

Cooked rice, for serving

1 green onion, thinly sliced, for garnish (optional)

Sesame seeds, for garnish (optional)

Place the Brussels sprouts and sweet potatoes in the bottom of a slow cooker. Drizzle with olive oil and salt and toss to coat. Cook on low for 2 to 3 hours until the potatoes are tender but not mushy.

30 minutes before serving, whisk together the soy sauce, hoisin sauce, vinegar, honey, ketchup, oil, garlic, ginger, cornstarch and chili paste. Pour over the vegetables. Toss to coat and adjust the seasoning if needed. Cover and cook on high for 30 minutes.

Serve with rice and sprinkle with green onions and sesame seeds, if desired.

ASIAN TOFU CABBAGE SALAD WITH MISO-GINGER DRESSING

This simple Asian-inspired salad makes a delicious and healthy lunch that is also great for entertaining and potlucks. It's a favorite I make often and I'll usually alternate the protein with whatever I have on hand. You can easily make the tofu and edamame beans ahead of time and store them overnight in the fridge. The bright, tangy, flavor-filled miso-ginger dressing goes perfectly with the crunchy cabbage and sweet mango.

YIELD: 4 SERVINGS

2 tbsp plus 2 tsp (40 ml) low sodium soy sauce, divided

5 tsp (35 g) honey, divided

4 garlic cloves, minced, divided

14 oz (400 g) extra-firm tofu, pressed, drained and cubed

1½ cups (300 g) fresh or thawed frozen shelled edamame beans

3 cups (300 g) Napa cabbage, thinly sliced

3 large green onions, thinly sliced

1 large mango, peeled, pitted, thinly sliced

1 tbsp (8 g) grated fresh ginger

5 tbsp (75 ml) rice vinegar

3 tbsp (42 g) miso paste, plus more to taste

2 tsp (10 ml) sesame oil

Sesame seeds, for serving (optional)

Roasted almond slices, for serving (optional)

Crushed raw ramen noodles, for serving (optional)

Add 2 tablespoons (30 ml) soy sauce, 2 teaspoons (14 g) honey and half the garlic to the bottom of your slow cooker, mixing well to combine. Toss in the tofu and edamame and turn to coat on all sides. Place the lid on top and cook on low for 2 to 3 hours or high for 1 hour.

Meanwhile, combine all the cabbage, green onion and mango in a large bowl. Whisk together the remaining garlic, ginger, vinegar, miso, remaining honey, sesame oil and remaining soy sauce and pour half over the salad, tossing to combine. Store in the fridge, covered, until ready to assemble.

Remove the tofu and edamame with a slotted spoon and layer over the salad. Serve with the remaining dressing drizzled over the top, toss again and sprinkle with sesame seeds, roasted almonds and crushed ramen noodles, if desired.

NOTE: To press the tofu, remove the tofu from the packaging and drain the water. Place the block between paper towels or a kitchen towel. Wrap firmly around the block and transfer to a plate. Top with another plate and place a heavy object (book, cans) on top of the plate. Allow tofu to press for 30 minutes to an hour. Drain and cut into small cubes.

CHINESE EGGPLANT WITH GARLIC SAUCE

My mom used to make this simple dish often when we were younger. At the time, I was not a fan of eggplant and would always try to sneak some onto my brothers' plates since they loved it. Now that I'm older, I actually love eggplant and this savory and slightly spicy version is similar to the one my mom used to make.

YIELD: 4 SERVINGS

½ cup (118 ml) water, plus more as needed

2 tbsp (30 ml) low sodium soy sauce

2 tbsp (32 g) vegetarian oyster sauce

1 tbsp (16 g) hoisin sauce

3 tsp (9 g) brown sugar or honey (21 g)

½–1 tsp red chili garlic paste or Sriracha, to taste (optional)

½ tsp sesame oil, plus more for garnish

4 garlic cloves, minced

1 tbsp (8 g) minced fresh ginger

2 lb (910 g) Chinese eggplant washed, cut into large chunks

1 tbsp (9 g) cornstarch

2 tbsp (30 ml) cold water

2 green onions, thinly sliced, divided

Sesame seeds, for garnish (optional)

In a medium bowl, mix the water, soy sauce, oyster sauce, hoisin sauce, brown sugar, chili paste, sesame oil, garlic and ginger together until combined for the sauce.

Add the eggplant to the bottom of the slow cooker and pour the sauce over the top, mixing well. Cook on high for 2 to 3 hours or on low for 4 to 5 hours. Add some more water as needed, depending on how hot your slow cooker runs.

To thicken the sauce, whisk together the cornstarch and cold water in a small bowl and stir into the slow cooker. Stir in half of the sliced green onions. Cover with the lid, turn the heat to high and allow the sauce to cook and thicken for 20 to 30 minutes.

Sprinkle with the remaining green onions, a drizzle of sesame oil and sesame seeds, if desired.

MANGO SESAME LENTIL LETTUCE WRAPS

These lettuce wraps make a fun and healthy weeknight meal. I love swapping in lentils for a meatless option.
They are a great protein source and are chock full of nutrients, folate and iron. Plus, they make a neutral
base for soaking up the sweet and savory hoisin sauce and balance wonderfully
with the crispy lettuce and sweet mango.

YIELD: 4 SERVINGS

½ cup (118 ml) low sodium soy sauce

¼ cup (55 g) hoisin sauce, plus more for topping

3 tbsp (63 g) honey

3 tbsp (45 ml) rice vinegar

3 tsp (15 ml) sesame oil

1 cup (200 g) dried green or brown lentils, rinsed and sorted through

2 garlic cloves, minced

2½ cups (591 ml) vegetable broth

2 cups (200 g) diced mango, fresh or frozen

1 red bell pepper, cored and finely chopped

1 head Boston or iceberg lettuce, leaves rinsed and patted dry

1 green onion, thinly sliced

Add the soy sauce, hoisin sauce, honey, vinegar, sesame oil, lentils and garlic to the slow cooker and stir to combine.

Pour in the vegetable broth, making sure the lentils are covered with liquid. Cook on high for 4 to 5 hours or on low for 7 to 8 hours.

Check once or twice during cooking and add water as needed. Toss in the mango and bell pepper and cook on high for 15 to 20 minutes.

Drain and fill the lettuce cups with a spoonful of filling and top with green onions and drizzle on more hoisin sauce, if needed.

MAPO TOFU (VEGETARIAN VERSION)

Mapo Tofu is one of our favorite dishes and although it's usually made with ground pork, my family enjoys this meatless version just as much. Shiitake mushrooms are used as a replacement to create this simple and satisfying meal.

YIELD: 6 SERVINGS

1 (14-oz [400-g]) package tofu, drained, pressed and cubed into ½" (1.2-cm) pieces

3 tbsp (45 ml) low sodium soy sauce

2 tbsp (30 ml) rice vinegar or apple cider vinegar

3 tbsp (48 g) tomato paste

1½ tbsp (24 g) black bean garlic sauce

1–2 tsp (5–10 g) red chili garlic paste, to taste

½ tsp ground Sichuan pepper or red pepper chili flakes (optional)

1 tsp brown sugar

1 cup plus 2 tbsp (267 ml) water, divided

2 tsp (10 ml) cooking oil

3 garlic cloves, minced

2–3 tsp (3–5 g) grated fresh ginger

6 dried shiitake mushrooms, sliced

2 tbsp (16 g) cornstarch

½ cup (50 g) fresh or frozen green peas, thawed

½ cup (50 g) fresh or frozen cubed carrots, thawed

½ tbsp sesame oil

Cooked rice, for serving

Add the tofu to the bottom of the slow cooker. In a small bowl, combine the soy sauce, vinegar, tomato paste, garlic sauce, chili paste, Sichuan pepper, sugar and 1 cup (237 ml) water.

Heat the oil in a skillet over medium-high heat. Sauté garlic, ginger and mushrooms for about 2 minutes, or until fragrant. Add the sauce and bring to a boil. Remove from the heat and pour the mixture into the slow cooker, covering the tofu. Cook on low for 3 to 4 hours or on high for 1 to 2 hours.

About 30 minutes before serving, whisk together the cornstarch and remaining water in a small bowl and stir into the slow cooker along with the peas and carrots. Turn the heat to high and cook for an additional 30 minutes or until the sauce thickens.

Stir in the sesame oil and serve with cooked rice.

NOTE: To press the tofu, remove the tofu from the packaging and drain the water. Place the block between paper towels or a kitchen towel. Wrap firmly around the block and transfer to a plate. Top with another plate and place a heavy object (book, cans) on top of the plate. Allow tofu to press for 30 minutes to an hour. Drain and cut into small cubes.

TERIYAKI PINEAPPLE PORTOBELLO BURGERS

Who doesn't love a good homemade burger? With the meaty texture of the portobello mushrooms, they make a filling and satisfying meal. The sweet teriyaki sauce complements the juicy pineapples and gets a kick of heat from the Sriracha mayo. These are so packed with flavor you won't even miss the meat!

YIELD: 4 SERVINGS

4 large portobello mushrooms

1 tbsp (8 g) minced fresh ginger

2 garlic cloves, minced

½ cup (118 ml) soy sauce

2 tbsp (25 g) brown sugar

2 tbsp (30 ml) mirin

1 tsp agave nectar or honey

4 whole wheat or Kaiser buns, toasted

4 lettuce leaves

1 large tomato, sliced ¼" (6-mm) thick

¼ cup (57 g) Sriracha mayonnaise

Wipe down the mushrooms with a clean, damp cloth. Then use a metal spoon to scrape the underside and remove the gills. In a large resealable container, combine the ginger, garlic, soy sauce, brown sugar, mirin and agave and place the mushrooms inside. Cover with the lid then give it a good shake. Marinate for at least 30 minutes to overnight, flipping the container so both sides get marinated.

Transfer the contents to a slow cooker and cook on low for 2 to 3 hours or on high for 1 to 2 hours. Remove and cut into slices.

To assemble, place a few mushroom slices amongst the toasted buns, and layer with lettuce, tomato and a drizzle of Sriracha mayo.

NOTE: To make Sriracha mayo, combine ½ cup (118 ml) mayonnaise with 2 tablespoons (30 ml) Sriracha.

THAI BASIL TOFU AND VEGETABLE RICE CASSEROLE

One thing I did not inherit from my mom was her green thumb. She has the most amazing garden and collection of fresh herbs. I love going over there during the summer and grabbing a bunch of Thai basil whenever I visit. It is completely different in taste from regular basil so the two cannot be interchanged in this case. It is my favorite herb to use in Asian cooking and the refreshing flavor along with the creamy coconut harmoniously balances out the heat from the green curry and chili flakes in this comforting casserole.

YIELD: 4 SERVINGS

1 cup (237 ml) boiling water

1 tbsp (16 g) green curry paste

1 cup (190 g) minute white rice

1 cup (75 g) dried shiitake mushroom slices, soaked and drained

2 garlic cloves, minced

1 tsp grated fresh ginger

1 medium onion, diced

1 tbsp (15 ml) fish sauce

14 oz (400 g) extra firm tofu, drained and pressed, cut into small cubes

1 red bell pepper, diced

1 small zucchini, diced

3 tbsp (45 ml) canned coconut milk

⅓ cup (10 g) chopped fresh Thai basil

1 tbsp (5 g) minced fresh cilantro

Lightly spray the inside of the slow cooker with non-stick cooking spray. Whisk in boiling water and green curry paste in the bottom until smooth. Toss in the rice, mushrooms, garlic, ginger, onion and fish sauce and stir to combine. Add the tofu and cook on high for 1½ to 2 hours, until rice is tender. Stir in the bell pepper, zucchini and coconut milk 20 minutes before serving. After 20 minutes, turn the power off and allow the casserole to rest for an additional 10 minutes, then add the fresh Thai basil and cilantro. Serve hot.

NOTE: To press the tofu, remove from the packaging and drain the water. Place the block between paper towels or a kitchen towel. Wrap firmly around the block and transfer to a plate. Top with another plate and place a heavy object (book, cans) on top of the plate. Allow the tofu to press for 30 minutes to an hour. Drain and cut into small cubes.

THAI RED CURRY VEGETABLES

This fragrant curry makes an easy and tasty meatless meal. Adding red curry paste is one of my favorite ways to spice up a veggie dish. It gives it that distinctive Thai flavor that we love and it actually gets my husband to happily skip the meat.

YIELD: 4 SERVINGS

2 cups (474 ml) vegetable broth

2 tbsp (32 g) red curry paste, to taste

1 tbsp (12 g) brown sugar or honey (21 g)

2 tsp (10 g) fish sauce

½ tbsp (8 ml) fresh lime juice

½ tbsp (4 g) freshly minced ginger

1 cup (100 g) baby corn, drained and cut in half

1 medium carrot, peeled, sliced in rounds

1 medium onion, cut into chunks

1 red bell pepper, cut into chunks

½ cup (165 g) cauliflower florets

1 (14-oz [400-g]) package extra-firm tofu, drained and cubed into ½" (1.2-cm) pieces

1 (14-oz [385-ml]) can coconut milk

1 cup (45 g) fresh chopped Thai basil

Cooked rice, for serving

1 tbsp (5 g) fresh chopped cilantro, for serving (optional)

Combine the vegetable broth, red curry paste, sugar, fish sauce and lime juice in the bottom of a 4- to 5-quart (3.8- to 4.7-L) slow cooker. Stir in the remaining ingredients up to, and including, the tofu. Cook on low for 6 to 8 hours. Twenty minutes before serving, add the coconut milk and Thai basil. Taste and adjust the seasonings.

Serve with rice and sprinkle with cilantro, if desired.

Sensational Soups

There is nothing more comforting to me than curling up with a warm bowl of soup, especially on a chilly day. It always reminds me of my mom. She is a soup fanatic and made the most flavorful soups, stews and curries that could just warm your soul.

Every night, she would make a different soup to serve alongside our meals. Even now, whenever I go over to her house, she always has a gigantic pot bubbling away.

Whether you're in the mood for Chinese Hot and Sour Soup (page 150) or Thai Butternut Squash Curry Soup (page 158), making them in the slow cooker means you can let them simmer all day long without having to spend a ton of time in the kitchen. Once it's ready, just grab your favorite spoon and sip away!

ASIAN BEEF STEW

Almost every family has their own version of a hearty beef stew. My parents made it nearly every other weekend, year round, but I crave it most once the weather turns cool. What sets this Asian Beef Stew apart from the North American and French versions is the additional layers of flavor from the lemongrass, star anise, ginger and other aromatics. It's cozy, comforting and will leave your home smelling amazing!

YIELD: 6–8 SERVINGS

2 lb (910 g) beef stew meat, trimmed and cut into 1–2″ (2–2.5 cm) chunks

⅓ cup (43 g) flour

1 tsp Chinese five-spice powder

1 tsp sea salt

½ tsp black pepper

2 tsp (10 ml) cooking oil

1 large onion, diced into large chunks

4 garlic cloves, minced

1 tbsp (15 ml) low sodium soy sauce

5 tbsp (80 g) tomato paste

4 cups (948 ml) beef broth

3 tsp (15 ml) fish sauce

1 tsp Madras curry powder

4 Russet potatoes, peeled and chopped into 1″ (2.5-cm) chunks

3 medium carrots, peeled and cut into 1″ (2.5-cm) chunks

1 whole star anise

French bread or cooked rice noodles, for serving

2 tbsp (10 g) coarsely chopped fresh cilantro, for garnish (optional)

In a large resealable bag, combine the beef, flour, five-spice, salt and pepper. Seal it closed and give it a good shake until well coated.

In a large skillet on medium-high heat, add the oil and brown the meat on all sides, about 3 to 4 minutes each. The meat will not be cooked through. Be careful not to crowd the skillet—you may have to work in batches. Transfer the browned beef into a 6-quart (5.7-L) slow cooker.

Return the skillet back to the stove and add the onion and garlic. Sauté for a minute or two then add the soy sauce and tomato paste until just hot enough to deglaze the pan, about 1 minute. Toss everything into the slow cooker over the beef. Add the broth, fish sauce, curry powder, potatoes, carrots and star anise to the cooker. Cook on low for 6 to 7 hours or on high for 3 to 4 hours, stirring halfway. Taste and season with salt as needed.

Ladle into bowls and serve with French bread or rice noodles and garnish with chopped cilantro, if desired.

CHINESE CHICKEN PORRIDGE (CONGEE)

Congee is a breakfast or lunch staple in many Asian families and there was always a big pot simmering on the stove when we were growing up. We call it *jook* and it was mainly rice, water or broth cooked down to a thick porridge that you can add various toppings to. It's the perfect comfort food when you're feeling sick or to warm you up on a cold day.

YIELD: 6 SERVINGS

1½ cups (95 g) uncooked jasmine or long grained rice

8 cups (1896 ml) low sodium chicken broth

2 cups (480 ml) water, plus more as needed

2″ (5-cm) knob ginger root, peeled and thinly sliced

1 cup (125 g) cooked chicken, shredded

⅛ tsp ground white pepper

Salt and pepper to taste

2 green onions, thinly sliced (optional)

Chopped fresh cilantro (optional)

Fried shallots (optional)

Low sodium soy sauce (optional)

Sesame oil (optional)

Add the rice to the bottom of a 6-quart (5.7-L) slow cooker. Pour in the broth, water and ginger. Cook on low for 5 to 6 hours or on high for 3 hours. Stir in the shredded chicken and season with salt, white and black pepper, to taste.

Serve in individual bowls topped with green onions, cilantro, fried shallots and a drizzle of soy sauce or sesame oil, if desired

CHICKEN LAKSA NOODLE SOUP

Chicken Laksa is a Malaysian soup made with coconut milk, vegetables and aromatic herbs and spices. We had this dish on our visit to Thailand and it was super comforting and full of complex and delicious flavors. The ingredient list might look long but it's really easy to make. Pan frying the curry paste beforehand brings out the deep and rich flavors. Laksa is a Malaysian curry paste that can be found in Asian supermarkets, or you can substitute with red Thai curry paste in a pinch.

YIELD: 4–5 SERVINGS

2 tsp (10 ml) cooking oil

½ cup (100 g) laksa paste (or red Thai curry paste)

3 garlic cloves, minced

1 tbsp (15 g) minced fresh ginger

1 medium onion thinly sliced

1 lb (455 g) boneless, skinless chicken thighs, chopped into thin slices

1 (14-oz [392-ml]) can coconut milk

4 cups (948 ml) low sodium chicken broth

3 tbsp (45 ml) fish sauce

1 cup (325 g) cauliflower florets

1 red bell pepper, cut into 1″ (2.5-cm) chunks

2 zucchini, cut into 1″ (2.5-cm) chunks

Juice and zest from 1 lime

6 oz (170 g) dried rice vermicelli noodles

Chopped fresh cilantro and Thai basil, for garnish (optional)

Cucumber, cut into thin matchsticks, for garnish (optional)

Lime wedges, for garnish (optional)

Mung bean sprouts, for garnish (optional)

Heat the oil in a skillet over medium-high heat and add the laksa paste and fry until aromatic, about a minute. Stir in the garlic, ginger, onion and chicken. Sauté for 2 minutes, just until aromatic. Stir in the coconut milk, chicken broth and fish sauce; bring to a boil then transfer to the slow cooker. Stir in the cauliflower and cook on low for 5 to 6 hours or on high for 3 to 4 hours. About 30 minutes before serving, stir in the bell peppers, zucchini and lime.

Prepare the noodles according to the package instructions and drain.

Divide the noodles among bowls and fill with the soup. Garnish with toppings of your choice.

CHINESE HOT AND SOUR SOUP

Hot and Sour Soup was always a favorite when we were growing up. My mom would load it up with traditional ingredients like wood ear fungus and lily buds, which I used to secretly pick out. Now that I make it for my own family, I swap those out for pantry-friendly baby corn and shiitake mushrooms instead. You still get the deep, rich flavors that are nutritious and satisfying.

YIELD: 4-5 SERVINGS

5 cups (1185 ml) chicken broth or vegetable broth

1 (14-oz [400-g]) package extra firm tofu, pressed, drained and cut into cubes

4 oz (112 g) shiitake mushrooms, thinly sliced

1 cup (131 g) thinly sliced bamboo shoots (fresh or canned, drained)

½ cup (90 g) canned baby corn, drained, cut into halves

3 garlic cloves, minced

2 tsp (3 g) fresh ginger, minced

3 tbsp (45 ml) rice vinegar or apple cider vinegar

1½ tbsp (22 ml) low sodium soy sauce

1 tsp dark soy sauce

½–1 tbsp (8–16 g) red chili garlic paste, to taste

½ tsp ground white pepper, plus more for serving

Salt to taste

2 tbsp (16 g) cornstarch

3 tbsp (45 ml) water

½ cup (63 g) shredded cooked chicken, optional

1 large egg, lightly beaten

Green onions, chopped for garnish (optional)

Thai red chilies, seeded and thinly sliced for garnish (optional)

Combine the broth, tofu, mushrooms, bamboo shoots, corn, garlic, ginger, vinegar, soy sauce and dark soy sauce into a slow cooker. Cook on low for 6 to 7 hours or on high for 3 to 4 hours. Add the chili paste, white pepper and salt to taste.

To thicken the soup, whisk together the cornstarch and water in a small bowl and stir into the slow cooker. Turn the heat to high and allow the soup to cook and thicken for 20 to 30 minutes. Stir in the shredded chicken and slowly pour the egg in a thin stream, while continuously stirring the soup, and allow the egg to cook, around 2 to 3 minutes.

Ladle into bowls and serve hot with green onions, sliced red chilies and additional white pepper, if desired.

KIMCHI JIGAE

Kimchi Jigae is a fiery Korean stew traditionally made with fermented kimchi, pork belly and tofu. It's hearty, comforting and can warm you up even on the most frigid day. I had a craving for this almost every week when I was pregnant with my son, and my sweet husband would pick up an order for me from the local Korean restaurant on the way back from work. Now, whenever I make this at home, I use a leaner cut of meat and load it up with extra veggies. It's the perfect dish to use up aged kimchi and makes a delicious and satisfying meal.

YIELD: 4–5 SERVINGS

1 tsp sesame oil

¼ lb (113 g) pork shoulder, trimmed of excess fat, sliced thinly

4 cups (400 g) kimchi (fully fermented), cut into bite-sized pieces

4 garlic cloves, minced

½ tsp minced fresh ginger

4 tbsp (60 ml) kimchi juice

½ tbsp (8 ml) Chinese rice wine or dry sherry

1½–2 tbsp (18–16 g) Korean red pepper paste (gochujang), to taste

½–1 tbsp (5–9 g) Korean chili powder (gochugaru), to taste

2 tsp (10 g) Korean soybean paste (doenjang)

5 cups (1185 ml) chicken broth

2 medium zucchini, diced (optional)

1 package of soft or medium tofu, sliced into 1″ (2.5-cm) cubes

Cooked rice, for serving

2 green onions, for garnish (optional)

Sesame seeds, for garnish (optional)

Heat the sesame oil in a skillet over medium-high heat. Add the pork and sauté for 2 minutes. Add the kimchi, garlic and ginger and sauté until it's fragrant and the kimchi is starting to get softer, about 2 minutes. Dump the contents of the skillet into the slow cooker.

Stir in the kimchi juice, wine, red pepper paste, chili powder and soybean paste. Slowly pour in the chicken broth and stir to combine well. Cook on low for 3 to 5 hours. Stir in the zucchini and tofu and cook on high for an additional 20 minutes.

Serve with cooked rice and garnish with green onions and sesame seeds, if desired.

NOTE: Kimchi, gochujang, gochugaru and doenjang can usually be found in most Asian supermarkets. Call ahead to be certain.

KOREAN PORK BONE SOUP (GAMJATANG)

Gamjatang is a traditional spicy soup made with pork, potatoes and hot peppers. It's the first Korean dish I learned how to make, as it was my husband's favorite soup. It does involve an extra step to parboil the bones, but the clear and flavorful broth it produces is well worth it. With the cold winters we get on the Mid-East coast, this comforting soup is like a warm umami hug for our bellies.

YIELD: 4–5 SERVINGS

9 pieces (614 g) pork neck bones

4 thin slices (8 g) of fresh ginger

¼ cup (3 g) dried shiitake mushrooms

1 tbsp (8 g) of minced ginger

1–2 dried red chili peppers

2 tbsp (32 g) Korean soybean paste (doenjang)

8 cups (1896 ml) water plus more as needed

6 garlic cloves, minced

3 tbsp (45 ml) fish sauce

3 tbsp (45 ml) Chinese rice wine, soju, or sake

1 tbsp (16 g) Korean red pepper paste (gochujang)

2 tbsp (32 g) Korean chili powder (gochugaru), to taste

4 large white potatoes, peeled, quartered

1 cup (340 g) Napa cabbage sliced in quarters

2 green onions, thinly sliced, divided

8 perilla leaves, sliced in thick strips, optional

Cooked rice, for serving

To parboil the bones, add them to a large stockpot and fill with water. Add ginger slices and bring to a boil then lower to medium heat and allow to simmer for 10 minutes. Skim out impurities with a fine mesh strainer or ladle. Drain and rinse the bones briefly under cool water, discard the ginger, then transfer bones to the bottom of a 6-quart (5.7-L) slow cooker.

Stir in the shiitake mushrooms, minced ginger, red chili peppers, soybean paste and water. Cover and cook on low for 3 to 4 hours, skimming off any excess fat. Stir in garlic, fish sauce, wine, red pepper paste, chili powder, potatoes, Napa cabbage, half of the green onions and the perilla leaves. Cover and cook on high for 1 hour, or until the potatoes are soft and the meat is tender but not falling off the bones.

Serve with rice or Korean *banchan* (side dishes) and garnish with remaining green onions.

NOTE: To thicken soup, mix together 3 tablespoons (28 g) cornstarch and 3 tablespoons (45 ml) cool water, stir the mixture into the soup and cook on high for about 30 minutes.

MISO SOUP WITH VEGETABLES AND SOBA NOODLES

When my husband and I visited Tokyo a few years ago, we had no idea we would be landing in the middle of typhoon season. It rained the entire time we were there but we didn't let that stop us from exploring the city. Whenever we got hungry, it wasn't hard to find a meal because there was a soup-and-noodle concoction on every corner. This version reminds me of the ones I had on our visit. It's a simple and comforting soup made with earthy miso, Napa cabbage, tofu and buckwheat soba noodles.

YIELD: 4–5 SERVINGS

½ cup (40 g) shiitake mushrooms, stemmed and sliced thin

1 carrot, peeled and sliced into rounds

½ cup (50 g) Napa cabbage, shredded

1 tbsp (15 g) minced garlic

1 tbsp (8 g) fresh ginger, sliced into rounds

½ tbsp (8 ml) low sodium soy sauce

2 tsp (10 ml) sesame oil

5 cups (1185 ml) chicken broth

¼ cup (55 g) miso paste

14 oz (400 g) extra-firm tofu, cut into ½" (1-cm) pieces

5 cups (1125 g) baby spinach

½ cup (76 g) shelled edamame

8 oz (210 g) cooked soba noodles, prepared according to package directions

Green onions, for garnish (optional)

Sesame seeds, for garnish (optional)

Combine the mushrooms, carrot, cabbage, garlic, ginger, soy sauce, sesame oil, broth and miso paste. Cook on low for 4 to 5 hours or on high for 2 to 3 hours. Add the tofu, spinach, edamame and cooked soba noodles and push down. Cover and allow to cook on high for 15 minutes. Do not overcook.

Ladle into noodle bowls and serve with green onions and sesame seeds, if desired.

NOTE: Serve with shredded precooked chicken or turkey, if desired.

THAI BUTTERNUT SQUASH CURRY SOUP

This is one of my favorite soups to make once the weather starts to get chilly. It's so healthy and full of nutrients from the butternut squash, sweet potatoes, fresh ginger and turmeric. The smooth, creamy texture and touch of heat with exotic flavors from the red curry paste is just enough to keep your spoon wandering back for more.

YIELD: 4–5 SERVINGS

5 cups (2250 g) butternut squash (or pumpkin), peeled and cubed

1 cup (200 g) sweet potatoes, peeled, roughly cubed

1 medium onion, peeled, diced

1 tbsp (8 g) fresh ginger, peeled

3 garlic cloves, sliced

3 cups (710 ml) chicken or vegetable broth

1 (13.5-oz [400-ml]) can coconut milk

½–1 tbsp (8–16 g) red curry paste, to taste

½ tsp turmeric

1 tbsp (15 ml) fresh lime juice

Salt and pepper, to taste

Drizzle of coconut milk, for garnish (optional)

Pumpkin seeds, for garnish (optional)

Chopped cilantro leaves, for garnish (optional)

Sliced red chili pepper, for garnish (optional)

Place the squash, sweet potatoes, onion, ginger, garlic and broth in a 4- to 5-quart (3.8- to 4.7-L) slow cooker. Cook on low for 6 to 8 hours or on high for 3 to 4 hours, until the squash and sweet potatoes are soft and cooked through.

Remove the lid and stir in the coconut milk, red curry paste, turmeric and lime juice. Allow the soup to cool slightly before puréeing. Using an immersion blender, purée directly in the slow cooker or pour contents into a blender and purée until smooth. Adjust seasonings as needed with salt and pepper.

Serve warm in bowls and garnish with a drizzle of coconut milk, pumpkin seeds, cilantro and sliced red chili pepper, if desired.

TOM YUM HOT AND SOUR SOUP

Tom Yum Soup is an extremely popular dish made with fragrant lemongrass, fresh galangal root, kaffir lime leaves and red chilies. It's deliciously nourishing and full of bold, sweet, sour and spicy flavors. It's one of the soups I turn to whenever I'm feeling under the weather or need something healthy and comforting. That punch of heat followed by its soothing flavors is sure to light up your taste buds.

YIELD: 4 SERVINGS

4 cups (948 ml) low sodium chicken broth

1" (2.5-cm) piece of galangal root or ginger root, thinly sliced

4 kaffir lime leaves, chopped (or 1 tbsp [15 ml] lime zest)

3 Thai red chilies, seeds removed, thinly sliced, to taste

2 stalks lemongrass, tough outer layer removed, chopped into thirds

½ lb (228 g) skinless chicken thighs or breast

2 tsp (10 g) Thai roasted chili paste (Nam Prik Prao) OR Tom Yum Paste, to taste

3 large dried shiitake mushrooms, soaked and drained

2 medium tomatoes, cut into quarters

½ lb (115 g) large uncooked shrimp, peeled and deveined, with tails intact

3½ tbsp (38 ml) lime juice

3 tbsp (45 ml) fish sauce

2 tsp (8 g) sugar

Chopped fresh cilantro leaves, for garnish

In a 4- to 5-quart (3.8- to 4.7-L) slow cooker, combine the broth, galangal, kaffir leaves, red chilies, lemongrass, chicken and chili paste. Cook on low for 6 to 7 hours or on high for 3 to 4 hours.

Transfer the chicken from the slow cooker, shred and return the chicken back to the soup.

Add mushrooms, tomatoes and shrimp and cook on high for an additional 20 to 25 minutes, or until the shrimp is opaque and pink. Season with lime juice, fish sauce and sugar, taste testing for a balance of sour, salty, sweet and spicy.

Serve warm in bowls and garnish with cilantro.

NOTE: If you are sensitive to spices, omit or reduce the amount of chilies and chili paste.

VIETNAMESE PHO BEEF RICE NOODLE SOUP

Pho holds the most coveted place in my foodie heart. It reminds me of my childhood and is the definition of soul food to me (much like chicken noodle soup is to many others) and is especially perfect on a cold or rainy day. I tweaked and converted my mom's family recipe into this slow-cooker version and it is still just as tasty. The key to developing the deep and rich flavors is to broil and toast the aromatics prior to adding them into the broth.

YIELD: 6–8 SERVINGS

1½ lbs (680 g) beef bones (a combination of marrow and knuckle)

½ lb (250 g) oxtail bones

3 star anise

2 green cardamom pods

1 tsp coriander seeds

1 tsp fennel seeds

4 whole cloves

½ medium yellow onion

1 (3″ [7.5-cm]) section of ginger, sliced in half

1 medium daikon, peeled, cut into 2″ (5-cm) pieces

1 carrot, peeled, cut into 2″ (5-cm) pieces

4 garlic cloves, minced

1 tbsp (12 g) kosher or sea salt, or to taste

2 tbsp (30 ml) fish sauce, or to taste

½ tbsp (6 g) sugar (granulated, yellow rock or palm)

2 cinnamon sticks

12 oz (340 g) fresh rice noodles or dried (banh pho) prepared according to directions on package

½ lb (228 g) flank, sirloin or top round, sliced very thinly across the grain

Fresh herbs: cilantro, mint, Thai basil

½ to 1 medium yellow onion, sliced paper thin, soaked in a bowl of cold water for 15 minutes

3 green onions, very thinly sliced

1–2 cups (50 g) fresh mung bean sprouts, washed, dried

Thai bird chilies, seeded, sliced

Lime wedges

Hoisin sauce or Sriracha

Place the beef and oxtail bones inside a large stockpot and fill to the top with water. Bring to a boil on high heat then lower to medium and allow to simmer for 10 minutes. Skim out impurities with a fine mesh strainer or ladle. Drain and rinse the bones briefly under cool water. Transfer the bones to the bottom of a 6-quart (5.7-L) slow cooker.

Heat a small frying pan on medium-low heat. Add star anise, cardamom, coriander and fennel and toast until fragrant, about 2 to 3 minutes. Place them in a cheesecloth and tie securely. Add to the slow cooker.

Stud the cloves into the onion and place it on an aluminum foil lined baking sheet with the ginger. Broil on high for 5 minutes, checking often, until lightly charred. Carefully transfer to the slow cooker.

Fill the slow cooker with enough fresh water to cover the bones and spices. Add daikon, carrot, garlic, salt, fish sauce, sugar and cinnamon sticks. Cook on high for 5 hours or on low for 8 hours. Taste and adjust seasonings as needed.

Skim off fat from the surface. Strain the broth with a fine mesh sieve into a large stockpot and discard the solids. Bring the pot to a boil.

Divide the cooked noodles among serving bowls. Top each with a few sliced raw sirloin pieces and ladle boiling broth over the top, cooking the meat.

Serve with fresh herbs, sliced onions, green onions, mung bean sprouts, chilies, lime wedges and sauces of your choice.

NOTE: Toasting the spices and broiling the onion brings out the maximum flavor for a rich and deep broth. You may skip these steps if in a hurry.

Delectable Desserts

My mom wasn't much of a baker when I was growing up but she always made us the prettiest bowls of fruit salads after dinner every night. To this day, my favorite desserts are fruit-based, but I do enjoy making decadent desserts for my husband who is a self-professed chocoholic. Making them in the slow cooker not only frees up the oven when you need it during the holidays, it's a great way to keep the house cool in the summer.

All of the desserts in this chapter have some sort of Asian twist to them and one of my favorites is the Mandarin Orange Cheesecake (page 166). Who knew the slow cooker could make such a silky, smooth cheesecake?

MANDARIN ORANGE CHEESECAKE

This silky cheesecake is light and refreshing with a cinnamon graham cracker crust that complements the hint of orange nicely. It's topped with a decorative layer of sliced oranges and the piped rosettes make this an impressive dessert to serve at any special occasion.

YIELD: 6–7 SERVINGS

1⅓ cups (300 g) graham cracker crumbs

6 tbsp (85 g) unsalted butter, melted

1½ tbsp plus ⅔ cup (168 g) sugar, divided

¼ tsp ground cinnamon

2 (8-oz [225-g]) packages cream cheese, softened

1 cup (230 g) sour cream

1 (11-oz [325-ml]) can Mandarin oranges, drained and juice reserved

2 tsp (10 ml) orange extract

2 eggs, lightly beaten

½ cup (55 g) whipped cream or buttercream frosting, for garnish (optional)

Line the bottom of a 6-inch (15-cm) springform pan with parchment paper. Place a double layer of heavy-duty foil and wrap securely around the pan. Place a steaming rack inside the slow cooker. If you don't have a steaming rack, make one by using a long piece of aluminum foil, scrunched up into a coil and formed into a figure eight or a circle large and strong enough to sit under the cake pan.

In a medium bowl, combine the graham cracker crumbs, melted butter, 1½ tablespoons (18 g) of sugar and cinnamon together. Press firmly into the bottom and sides of the springform pan.

In a large bowl, mix the cream cheese and remaining sugar together until smooth. Add the sour cream and 2 tablespoons (30 ml) reserved orange juice and the orange extract and mix until combined. Beat in the eggs one by one until smooth. Pour into the prepared springform pan, then place the pan on top of the coil. Lay two paper towels over the slow cooker and place the lid securely on top.

Cook on high until the cheesecake is set, but slightly soft in the center, around 2 hours. Turn off the heat and allow the cheesecake to stand, covered, in the slow cooker for 1 hour. The cheesecake will set and the top will appear dull.

Remove the pan from the slow cooker and cool for 1 hour on a wire rack. Refrigerate the cheesecake covered, 8 hours or overnight. Decorate with orange slices and pipe on rosettes with whipped cream or buttercream frosting.

ASIAN PEAR PUDDING CAKE

Asian Pears were one of my favorite fruits when I was younger. As soon as they were in season, my mom would buy a ton and we'd have one after dinner every night. They are sweet, crunchy and have a delicate taste when you add them to desserts. This bread pudding cake makes a comforting sweet treat and leaves your house smelling amazing!

YIELD: 10 SERVINGS

2 cups (250 g) all-purpose flour

⅔ cup plus ¼ cup (205 g) sugar, divided

3 tsp (9 g) baking powder

¼ tsp salt

½ cup (58 g) unsalted butter, cold, and cut into ½" (1.2-cm) cubes

1 cup (237 ml) almond milk

2 medium Asian pears (or Bosc pears), divided, ⅔ cut into chunks and the remaining ⅓ cut into slices, for topping

½ cup (118 ml) apple juice

½ cup (170 g) honey

2 tbsp (28 g) butter, melted

½ tsp ground cinnamon

Line a 9 × 5-inch (23 × 13-cm) loaf pan with parchment paper and set aside. In a small bowl, combine the flour, ⅔ cup (150 g) sugar, baking powder and salt. Using two forks, cut in the cold butter until the mixture resembles coarse crumbs. Stir in the milk until just moistened. Spread the batter into a prepared pan; sprinkle the chopped pears evenly over the batter.

In another small bowl, whisk together the apple juice, honey, melted butter, cinnamon and the remaining sugar. Pour over the pears. Place the pan in the slow cooker (without a rack). Cover and cook on high for 2 hours. Top with sliced pears and cook for an additional 30 minutes to 1 hour until the pears are softened.

BLACK SESAME BROWNIES

Brownies are my husband's favorite dessert, especially when they are chocolatey and fudgy.
These have a hint of black sesame powder which adds a delicious rich and nutty undertone.

YIELD: 10 SERVINGS

1 cup (125 g) all-purpose flour

¼ cup (30 g) unsweetened cocoa powder

2 tsp (5 g) black sesame powder or finely ground black sesame seeds

¾ tsp baking powder

¼ tsp salt

½ cup (58 g) unsalted butter

½ cup (90 g) semi-sweet chocolate chips

1 cup (225 g) sugar

3 large eggs, lightly beaten

1 tsp pure vanilla extract

½ cup (90 g) semi-sweet mini chocolate chips, plus more for topping, if desired

Take a long piece of aluminum foil and fold it lengthwise into a long strip. Press it along the inside perimeter of your slow cooker, creating a ring. This will prevent the edges from burning. Next, line the bottom with a piece of parchment, leaving an overhang on the sides for easier removal.

In a small bowl, whisk together the flour, cocoa powder, sesame powder, baking powder and salt.

Place the butter and chocolate chips in a medium microwave-safe bowl. Heat on high power for 30-second increments, stirring well after each, until completely smooth and melted. Whisk in the sugar until smooth. Beat in the eggs, one by one, then add the vanilla.

Slowly stir in the flour mixture until just combined; do NOT overmix. Fold in the mini chocolate chips. Pour the batter into the lined slow cooker and smooth out using a rubber spatula. Top with additional chocolate chips if desired.

Cover the slow cooker with a double layer of paper towels then place the lid securely over the towels. This prevents any water from dripping into the cake batter.

Cook on low for 2½ to 3 hours, then remove the cover and cook for an additional 10 to 15 minutes. Remove the insert from the slow cooker and allow to cool completely. Lift the parchment paper to remove the brownies and slice into squares.

CHINESE STEAMED SPONGE CAKE

This sponge cake is a classic Chinese dessert that my mom used to make when we were younger. She was not much of a baker, but this simple recipe was one of her specialties that she learned to make just for us. The cake is steamed instead of baked, which helps it stay fluffy and moist without having any butter. It's lightly sweetened with a hint of vanilla, so it makes a great breakfast or a snack on the go.

YIELD: 6 SERVINGS

1 cup (115 g) sifted cake flour

1 tsp baking powder

⅛ tsp salt

5 large eggs, room temperature

1 tsp pure vanilla extract

1 cup (225 g) sugar

Pour 1 inch (2.5 cm) of water into a 6-quart (5.7-L) slow cooker. Place a steamer rack in the bottom. If you don't have a steamer rack, make one using a long piece of aluminum foil, scrunched up into a coil and formed into a figure eight or a circle large and strong enough to sit under the cake pan.

Lightly coat an 8-inch (20-cm) round cake pan with non-stick cooking spray and line the bottom with parchment paper.

In a medium bowl, whisk together the sifted flour, baking powder and salt. Set aside.

Using a stand mixer or a hand mixer on high speed, beat the eggs until they are light and foamy, about 1 minute. Slowly blend in the vanilla and sugar and continue beating until the mixture thickens and the volume increases, about 5 to 7 minutes.

Gradually fold in the flour mixture until just combined. Pour the batter into the prepared pan and carefully place on top of the coil. Cover the slow cooker with a double layer of paper towels then place the lid securely over the towels. This prevents any water from dripping into the cake batter. Cook covered on high for 1½ to 2 hours, or until a toothpick inserted in the middle comes out clean. Allow the cake to cool in the pan for 5 minutes before removing and serve warm or cool.

GINGER TEA POACHED PEARS

I adore pears. They are light, juicy and refreshing. We usually enjoy them straight from the bowl but they also make exquisite desserts when you poach them with fragrant jasmine tea and spices.

YIELD: 4–6 SERVINGS

1 jasmine or green tea bag, or loose leaves

5 cups (1200 ml) water

1 cup (340 g) honey, plus more for topping

½" (1 cm) of fresh ginger, peeled and sliced

2 cinnamon sticks

1 whole star anise

6 medium Bosc pears, cored, peeled and left whole

In a small mug, steep the tea in ½ cup (118 ml) of boiling water for at least 10 minutes. Strain the tea into a 4- to 5-quart (3.8- to 4.7-L) slow cooker. Add the water, honey, ginger, cinnamon and star anise. Stir to blend. Place the pears upright in the tea mixture.

Cook covered for 3 to 4 hours on low or on high for 2 hours, until the pears are almost tender. Using a slotted spoon, transfer the pears onto a plate to cool. Drizzle with some remaining liquid or honey, if desired.

LUNAR NEW YEAR SWEET RICE CAKE (NIAN GO)

Nian Go is a traditional steamed rice cake that is usually made around Lunar New Year. My mom used to pan-fry the slices for a crispy coating but my brothers and I loved them both ways and always looked forward to this sweet and sticky treat. This rice cake symbolizes good luck and prosperity. It is usually garnished with red dates for added color and a festive touch and goes perfectly with a hot cup of green tea.

YIELD: 6 SERVINGS

1 cup plus ¾ cup (414 ml) water, divided

½" (1 cm) fresh ginger, thinly sliced

1 cup (200 g) dark brown sugar

½ tsp ground allspice

2 cups (300 g) glutinous rice flour

¾ cups (115 g) rice flour

2 tsp (10 ml) vanilla extract

½ tbsp (8 ml) molasses

1 tbsp (6 g) orange zest

1 tsp vegetable oil

2 Chinese dried dates (jujubes), for garnish (optional)

Sesame seeds, for garnish (optional)

Fill a 6-quart (5.7-L) slow cooker with 1 inch (2.5 cm) of water. Place a steaming rack inside. If you don't have a steaming rack, make one using a long piece of aluminum foil, scrunched up into a coil and formed into a figure eight or a circle large and strong enough to sit under the cake pan.

Lightly coat an 8-inch (20-cm) round foil pan with non-stick cooking spray or line an 8-inch (20-cm) cake pan with parchment paper on the bottom.

In a medium saucepan, add 1 cup (237 ml) of water and ginger and bring to a boil. Lower the heat to medium-low and allow to simmer for 10 minutes. Turn off the heat, and stir in brown sugar and allspice until the sugar is completely dissolved. Remove the ginger slices and add the remaining water, to cool down the mixture.

In a large mixing bowl, combine the flours together then slowly stir in the brown sugar mixture until the batter is smooth. Add vanilla extract, molasses, orange zest and vegetable oil and mix until thoroughly combined. The batter should be the consistency of a pourable caramel sauce. Add more water as needed, 1 to 2 tablespoons (15 to 30 ml) at a time. Pour the batter into the prepared pan and gently tap on the counter to release any air bubbles.

Place the pan on top of the foil rack. Cover the slow cooker with a double layer of paper towels and place the lid securely on top. Cook covered on high for 2 to 3 hours, until the cake is very firm to the touch, checking every hour and replenishing the water as needed. While the cake is warm, garnish with dates and sesame seeds, if desired. Allow the cake to cool in the pan on the wire rack. Cut into slices and serve.

MANGO COCONUT TAPIOCA PUDDING

Tapioca pudding is a fun dessert that's popular in Asia. It's made with small, chewy tapioca pearls cooked in a sweet and creamy coconut milk custard. Chunky fresh mango makes this a light and refreshing treat.

YIELD: 6 SERVINGS

1 tsp coconut oil

2 (14-oz [400-ml]) cans coconut milk

¾ cup (144 g) coconut sugar or granulated sugar

⅔ cup (90 g) small tapioca pearls

1 large egg

1 tsp pure vanilla extract

1 tsp lime juice

2 cups (180 g) diced mango, fresh or frozen, divided

Shredded unsweetened coconut, toasted

Grease the inside of the slow cooker with coconut oil. Add the coconut milk, coconut sugar and tapioca pearls and stir to combine. Cook on low for 2 to 3 hours, until the pearls have become transparent.

In a medium bowl, lightly beat the egg and scoop out ¼ cup (59 ml) of warm tapioca mixture and pour over the egg. Whisk until combined and pour the egg mixture into the slow cooker, mixing well with the tapioca pudding. Stir in the vanilla and lime juice. Cover and cook on low for 30 minutes and then turn off. Stir in ½ cup (45 g) of the mango chunks and allow the pudding to rest and set for 30 minutes.

Serve layered in individual glass jars or in bowls topped with the remaining diced mango and toasted coconut.

MATCHA GREEN TEA CAKE

I am a big tea drinker and love the taste of matcha, a traditional Japanese green tea powder. Its rich and sweet flavor make it superb for adding to drinks and baked goods. This cake is soft, fluffy and coated with a creamy frosting and makes a delightful dessert or afternoon snack.

YIELD: 1 LOAF

1½ cups (173 g) sifted cake flour

1 tbsp (9 g) matcha green tea powder

1 tsp baking powder

⅛ tsp salt

10 tbsp plus ¼ cup (185 g) unsalted butter, room temperature, divided

2⅔ cups (335 g) powdered sugar, divided

3 large eggs, room temperature

½ cup (122 g) plain yogurt, room temperature

½ tsp pure vanilla extract

½ tsp rose extract

1–2 tbsp (15–30 ml) milk

Grease a 9 × 5-inch (23 × 13-cm) loaf pan with butter or non-stick cooking spray and line with parchment paper, cut to fit.

In a large bowl, whisk together the flour, green tea powder, baking powder and salt until combined.

Using a stand mixer or a hand mixer on medium, cream 10 tablespoons (156 g) butter and 1⅓ cups (300 g) sugar together until light and fluffy, about 3 minutes. Add in the eggs, one at a time, beating well after each addition and scraping the bowl clean, as needed. Beat in the yogurt and vanilla until smooth and fold in the flour mixture with a spatula until just combined.

Pour the batter into the prepared loaf pan and place inside the bottom of a large 6-quart (5.7-L) slow cooker. Cover and cook on high until a toothpick inserted in the center of the cake comes out clean, about 1 to 1½ hours. Cool in the pan on the wire rack for 10 minutes, then remove it from the pan carefully. Pull off the parchment and cool completely.

In a large bowl using an electric hand mixer, cream the remaining butter on medium speed until light and fluffy, about 3 minutes. Slowly add the remaining powdered sugar and rose extract and beat until smooth. Add the milk, 1 tablespoon (15 ml) at a time, until the desired consistency is reached. Spread over the cooled cake with an offset spatula.

SWEET GREEN BEAN SOUP

This delectable soup is a traditional Chinese dessert that is served warm in the winter and chilled during the summer. It's slightly sweetened with raw sugar and the flavors are brightened up with a hint of citrus.

YIELD: 4–6 SERVINGS

½ cup (100 g) green mung beans, soaked for 2 hours, rinsed and drained

4 cups (948 ml) water

2 pieces dried tangerine peel (optional)

½ cup (100 g) Chinese rock sugar (or raw turbinado sugar)

Canned coconut milk, for serving

1 tbsp (14 g) barley (optional)

1 tbsp (14 g) cooked tapioca pearls (optional)

1 tbsp (14 g) cooked sago (optional)

Place the beans, water and tangerine peel inside a 6-quart (5.7-L) slow cooker. Cover with the lid and cook on high for 3 hours or on low for 6 hours.

Add the sugar and test for desired level of sweetness before adding more. Cover and cook for an additional 30 minutes.

Ladle into serving bowls and stir in 1 to 2 tablespoons (15 to 30 ml) coconut milk and any additional add-ins, if desired.

THAI COCONUT STICKY RICE WITH MANGO

This is a popular Thai dessert made with sticky rice, coconut and sweet mangoes. The light and refreshing flavors make this a delightful treat to enjoy on a warm day.

YIELD: 6 SERVINGS

1½ cups (300 g) glutinous rice, soaked overnight in water, rinsed and drained

3 cups (711 ml) water

1½ cups (355 ml) canned coconut milk

⅔ cup (135 g) coconut sugar or brown sugar

¼ tsp salt

3 large mangoes, cut into slices or chunks, for serving

Toasted coconut chips, for serving (optional)

Grease a 6-quart (5.7-L) slow cooker with non-stick cooking spray. Add the drained rice and water to the slow cooker and stir to combine. Cover and cook on high for 3 hours or on low for 6 hours.

While the rice is cooking, heat the coconut milk in a saucepan over medium heat. Add sugar and salt then bring to a boil, continuously stirring until the sugar is dissolved. Remove from the heat and cover with the lid to keep warm.

Transfer the cooked rice to a large bowl. Stir in 1 cup (237 ml) of the heated coconut milk with the glutinous rice. Cover the bowl with plastic wrap and allow to stand for 30 minutes until the milk has been absorbed slightly. Serve in individual bowls with a drizzle of reserved coconut milk and top with mango and coconut chips.

Slow Cooker Basics

Slow cookers can be a very valuable and convenient kitchen tool for busy cooks. I've tried more than a dozen over the years and now have five that I use regularly to help me fix dinner and plan ahead for the week.

They have come a long way since they were first introduced by Rival back in 1971. These days, you can find them in a range of colors and sizes along with many modern features.

The recipes in this book were developed and tested to satisfy 4 to 6 people using a 4-, 5- or 6-quart (3.8-, 4.7- or 5.7-L) slow cooker with a removable insert.

If you are cooking for fewer people, the recipes may be halved to serve 2 or 3, in which case you can use a smaller size slow cooker.

No matter what size you plan to purchase, on the next page I have included a guide to slow cooker sizes based on how many people you are feeding.

SLOW COOKER SIZE	FOR
1½ quart (1.4 L)	1 person—great for dips and sauces
2 quart (1.9 L)	2 people—great for appetizers or dinners for 2 with no leftovers
3½ to 4 quart (3.3 to 3.8 L)	3 to 4 people—great for small family-favorite meals such as chili and stews
5 quart (4.7 L)	Large family of 5 to 7—great for family-sized dinners with leftovers
6 quart (5.7 L)	Large family of 8 or more—great for potluck or dinner with guests

COOKING TIME

All slow cookers cook differently so it is important to get to know your slow cooker and see how it compares.

The cooking times listed in this book are a range, so it's always a good idea to check on your food a little before the minimum cooking time to test for doneness.

Many older models tend to cook at lower temperatures than the newer models do. The new low is almost as hot as the old high so please refer to your owner's manual for proper use and care of your slow cooker. If your slow cooker runs on the hotter side, you may need to add more liquid to make up for the extra evaporation. If you have an older model that runs on the lower side, my recipes that call for cornstarch to thicken sauces may not set properly. In that case, spoon out all the sauce from the slow cooker into a small saucepan and bring to a boil on high heat until it thickens up. For other recipes, you may need to increase the cooking times and use less liquid.

The various temperature settings used will depend on how far in advance you are able to cook your food. Slow cooking on low allows flavors to develop, meats to become tender and sauces to thicken. Foods cooked on high will be ready sooner, but also might taste watery and boiled.

When in doubt, cook a recipe on low so that there is no risk of overcooking. You can always turn the temperature to high at the end if the food is not fully cooked.

The following chart helps to compare cooking times for high, medium and low settings:

HIGH	MEDIUM	LOW
1–2 hours	2–3 hours	3–5 hours
3–4 hours	4–5 hours	5–7 hours
5–6 hours	6–7 hours	7–9 hours
7–8 hours	8–9 hours	9–11 hours

BROWNING

Some recipes call for browning or sautéing ingredients before placing them in the slow cooker. This extra step adds a rich caramel layer, color, texture and enhances the flavor, which is essential to reach maximum results and stay true to the authenticity of the dish.

However, if you are in a hurry or just need to keep things simple, feel free to skip this step and add all the ingredients directly into the slow cooker.

If you have a slow cooker that has the searing option or a multicooker, you can skip the stove and brown your food directly in the pot.

An electric water boiler can also be used to soften up vegetables prior to adding them into the slow cooker.

CUTS OF MEAT

The best cuts of meat suited for slow cooking are often the less expensive and fattier versions. Chuck roasts, pork shoulders, briskets, lamb shanks, short ribs, chicken thighs and drumsticks are great choices—just be sure to trim off the excess fat.

It's also best to not use frozen food.

LAYERING

For even cooking, cut food into uniform-size pieces. Place firm, slow-cooking root vegetables (like potatoes and carrots) at the bottom of the slow cooker and toss the meat on top.

BRANDS

With so many slow cookers on the market, it's hard to know which one to choose. This will depend on your budget ($20 to $400), how many people you will be cooking for (1½ to 7 quarts [1.4 to 6.6 L]), countertop space, what features you want and the design.

Here are a few popular ones on the market today. I've had a chance to test out some of them and am sharing my thoughts on each, but as always, be sure to shop around and do your own research to see which one YOU think will work best for your needs:

Crock-Pot® Smart-Pot® 4-Quart Digital Slow Cooker is a mid-size programmable slow cooker with a flat digital panel, various time selections and an automatic shift-to-warm setting. I use this slow cooker to make a lot of medium batch recipes. It's easy to use and very reasonably priced.

Crock-Pot® 6-Quart Programmable Cook and Carry™ Slow Cooker has an easy locking lid gasket for extra-seal and an Easy Smart-Pot pre-set control and shifts to automatic warm setting once the food is cooked. The 6-quart (5.7-L) capacity is great for large batches of soups and stews. It's easy to use and priced reasonably.

Cuisinart® 3.5-Quart Programmable Slow Cooker has a 24-hour LCD countdown timer, touchpad control panel, four cooking modes including automatic keep-warm, and stay-cool handles for safety. This compact-sized slow cooker is a great option when making meals for a couple or a small family. It heats up quickly and is priced at the mid-high price range for its size.

Hamilton Beach® Programmable 5-Quart Slow Cooker has an easy-clean touch pad and automatically shifts to warm once the food is cooked. This is the slow cooker I use on a daily basis. The 5-quart (4.7-L) insert makes this the ideal size for a family of four with enough for leftovers the next day. The price is very reasonable and is a good choice for a reliable slow cooker.

Hamilton Beach® Set and Forget® Slow Cooker is a versatile programmable 6-quart (5.7-L) slow cooker with probe and manual mode. It automatically shifts to warm once the food is cooked and travels well with a lid that clips into place. The mid-range price is reasonable for its quality and features.

KitchenAid® 4-Quart Multi-Cooker is an all-in-one cooking system with a digital display of over 10 settings including sear, sauté, rice, simmer, yogurt, boil, steam, risotto and slow cook. It has a 24-hour keep-warm setting and a dual purpose steam basket and roasting rack. This is the higher-end price point, but we were fans of the modern design, ease of use and all the bells and whistles it came with. It makes a great option for those with limited space.

KitchenAid® 6-Quart Slow Cooker is a 24-hour programmable slow cooker, with 4 temperature settings including "medium" for more control and automatically switches to the keep-warm setting after cooking is done. This is the 6-quart (5.7-L) slow cooker I most often use when I'm recipe-testing large batches of soups, curries and stews. It cooks evenly and the digital display and timer are extremely easy to use. This has a mid-high price-point but is very reasonable for the quality, size and features. The attractive design also makes this earn a permanent spot on our kitchen counter.

The Ninja® Cooking System is a 3-in-1 cooking system with settings for steaming, roasting, and browning. It also comes with a roasting rack and can be programmed to cook for up to 12 hours. It has an automatic keep-warm option as well as a buffet setting. It's also priced on the higher end, but is an option to look into for the included features.

USING YOUR SLOW COOKER

• In order to operate correctly, a slow cooker typically needs to be filled at least halfway and no more than two-thirds full.

• Serve SAFE food: To keep food safe, remove the contents of the slow cooker within an hour of thoroughly cooking, and then refrigerate the leftovers. Don't reheat food in the slow cooker; it's better to use the stove or microwave to heat then add back to the slow cooker. Avoid opening the lid repeatedly because you will release steam which may add 20 or so minutes to your cooking time, so no peeking unless instructed by the recipe!

• Avoid using frozen food unless they are prepackaged slow-cooker meals sold in the freezer case. Be sure your meat is fully thawed before turning your slow cooker on.

• Remember to coat the slow cooker insert with a non-stick cooking spray prior to adding food in order to avoid sticking—particularly for casseroles and stews.

• Avoid overcrowding and fill the slow cooker half to two-thirds full.

• Use a thermometer: check the doneness of food at the beginning of the recommended time for the temperature setting and allow to cook longer as needed.

Stocking Your Pantry for Asian Cooking

Having a well-stocked pantry is essential for whipping up your favorite Asian meals at home. We moved to a small town a few years ago and I was thrilled that I was still able to find most of the ingredients I need to make the dishes we love.

Most major grocery stores have an international section and nowadays, they are stocked with a number of the key ingredients to get you started.

These make up the backbone of many of your favorite Asian recipes so that you can use them again and again.

For anything beyond the staples, and for anything harder to find, you can shop online or stop off at your nearest Asian supermarket.

It might seem intimidating if you don't know what to look for, so I've compiled this key ingredient list and an alphabetical list of the standard and unconventional ingredients that I used for the recipes in this book.

The seven ingredients that I reach for most often whenever I am making anything Asian-inspired are fish sauce, hoisin sauce, oyster sauce, red chili garlic paste, rice vinegar, soy sauce and Sriracha.

They all can be found at most major grocery stores, online and in Asian supermarkets. Just call ahead to be sure.

BLACK BEAN PASTE / SAUCE / GARLIC SAUCE

A sweet and savory paste made from fermented and salted black soybeans, garlic and soy sauce used in a variety of stir-fries, braised meats or in marinades. They can be found in some major grocery stores, Asian supermarkets and online.

RED CHILI GARLIC PASTE (SAMBAL OELEK)

A spicy, garlicky condiment made from ground chili, garlic, rice wine vinegar and salt used in Thai, Vietnamese and Chinese cooking. Adds flavor and spice to noodles and fried rice and can be used as a dipping sauce. It can be found in some major grocery stores, Asian supermarkets and online.

CILANTRO

This herb is used frequently in Asian cooking to add freshness and flavor to curries, sauces, marinades and salads. It can be found in major grocery stores and Asian supermarkets.

COCONUT MILK

Canned coconut milk is very popular in Southeast Asian dishes. It adds a creamy thickness and balances the flavors of soups and curries. It can be found in major grocery stores.

DOENJANG

Korean fermented soybean paste is an essential ingredient in many Korean dishes. It adds a salty, earthy and savory flavor and can be found at most Asian supermarkets and online.

DRIED WHOLE RED CHILI PEPPERS

Whole Thai chili peppers that have been preserved by sun-drying them. They are spicy and used a lot in Asian cooking as a replacement and/or in addition to fresh chilies. These can be found in Asian supermarkets and online.

FERMENTED SPICY BEAN PASTE

A spicy and savory condiment made from a mixture of broad beans and chili fermented together. It's used in a variety of dishes and adds a fiery and deep complex umami flavor to stir-fries, marinades, soups and more. This can be found in most Asian supermarkets and online.

FISH SAUCE

An essential ingredient used in Thai and Vietnamese cooking made from fermented fish and salt. It has a pungent smell but adds intense depth and umami flavor to any dish. This can be found in some major grocery stores, Asian supermarkets and online.

FIVE-SPICE POWDER

A blend of cinnamon, cloves, fennel, star anise and Sichuan peppercorns. A strong, flavorful mixture of five spices that give the sweet, sour, pungent, bitter and salty flavors found in Chinese cooking. Used to marinate meats, poultry and stir-fries. It can be found at major grocery stores.

GALANGAL ROOT

A root used in many Thai dishes that often gets confused with ginger, however, they are not the same and it tastes more like pepper. It can be found in most Asian supermarkets.

GINGER, GARLIC, GREEN ONIONS

These aromatic ingredients are quintessential to Asian cooking. They are known as the flavor trifecta and add freshness and flavor to any dish. They can be found in major grocery stores and Asian supermarkets.

GOCHUGARU

Korean chili powder (aka Korean chili flakes, hot pepper flakes and red pepper flakes) is a very commonly used ingredient in Korean cuisine. The spice level varies for various brands but it is less spicy than the Thai chilies with a slightly sweet undertone. This can be found in some Asian supermarkets and online.

GOCHUJANG

A commonly used Korean chili paste made with glutinous rice, fermented soybeans, salt and sweeteners. It is savory and spicy and can be used in marinades, stews and dipping sauces. This can be found in some Asian supermarkets and online.

HOISIN SAUCE

A thick, sweet, tangy and smoky sauce used in a lot of marinades, stir-fries and alone as a dipping sauce. It is often confused with oyster sauce but both are quite different with distinct flavors. It is a popular sauce that can be found in many major grocery stores.

KAFFIR LIME LEAVES

The leaves from kaffir limes add a bold citrus flavor in Thai and Vietnamese dishes. They can be found in the herb section in most Asian supermarkets.

KIMCHI

A traditional fermented Korean side dish most commonly made with a variety of seasonings from Napa cabbage, radish, green onions or cucumber. This can be found in most Asian supermarkets in the refrigerator section.

LAKSA PASTE

A mild curry used in many Malaysian and Singaporean dishes consisting mainly of shrimp paste, lemongrass, galangal and red chili. It can be found in most Asian supermarkets and online.

LEMONGRASS

This grassy herb is used in many Asian dishes to add a mildly sweet and potent lemon flavor. It can be found in most Asian supermarkets.

MIRIN

A Japanese rice wine that adds a mild sweetness and aroma to dishes. It also helps to add luster to sauces. It can be found in most Asian supermarkets or online. Add sugar to dry sherry or white wine as a substitute.

MISO PASTE

A traditional Japanese seasoning made from fermented soybean paste that is used to add depth and umami flavor to soups, sauces, marinades and dressings. A variety of Miso (red, white and yellow) can be found in most Asian supermarkets in the refrigerator section or online.

NOODLES

Noodles are a staple in Asian cuisine. There are tons of varieties and I like to keep a various stock on hand for different dishes. Rice noodles, bean thread, wheat, soba, ramen, somen, udon, egg, etc. They can be found at most major grocery stores, Asian supermarkets and online.

OYSTER SAUCE

An essential ingredient used in many Asian stir-fries, noodle and vegetable dishes. It has a rich, savory and slightly sweet undertone and adds color and flavor. It can be found at some major grocery stores, Asian supermarkets and online.

Vegetarian Oyster Sauce is made from dried mushroom extract and makes a suitable substitute for regular oyster sauce with its similar taste and texture. It can be found in most Asian supermarkets and online.

PERILLA LEAVES

Perilla leaves are a member of the mint family and are usually added to savory Korean dishes and soups. They can be found at some Asian supermarkets.

PLUM SAUCE

A popular sweet and tangy sauce used in marinades, dips and sauces. This can be found in most major grocery stores and all Asian supermarkets.

RICE

A staple accompaniment to all Asian cuisines. A variety of short grain, long grain and brown rice can be found at all major grocery stores.

RICE PAPER

Among one of the staples in a Vietnamese kitchen. It is made with rice flour and tapioca powder and is used to wrap summer and spring rolls. It can be found in some major grocery stores, Asian supermarkets and online.

RICE VINEGAR OR RICE WINE VINEGAR (UNSEASONED)

A slightly milder and less acidic vinegar made from fermented glutinous rice. It's used for pickling and adds a tangy flavor to marinades, sauces, vinaigrettes and dipping sauces. Use half the amount called for with cider or distilled vinegar as a substitute. This can be found in most grocery stores and all Asian supermarkets.

SOY SAUCE

An absolute staple in Chinese and Asian cooking. It's an all-purpose seasoning made from fermented soybeans, wheat, water and salt. It comes in light and dark varieties as well as low sodium, which is what I use most often. It adds that unique savory flavor to any dish, including stir-fries, marinades and dipping sauces. This popular ingredient can be found in almost every major grocery store.

Dark soy sauce is thicker, darker in color and slightly sweeter from the added molasses. I use a combination of both soy sauces to enhance the flavor of stir-fries, braised meats and stews, but if you can't find it or have a limited amount of pantry space, feel free to skip this purchase. It can be found in Asian supermarkets or online.

Tamari is made without wheat so it is suitable for those looking for a gluten-free option, however, it is always important to check the labels to be safe. Tamari has a lighter taste so you may have to adjust the seasonings as needed before serving. It can be found in some major grocery stores, Asian supermarkets or online.

SRIRACHA

A popular spicy, fiery hot sauce made from a blend of fresh chilies, dried chilies and vinegar. It can be found at most major grocery stores, Asian supermarkets and online.

STAR ANISE

A spice commonly used in Asian cuisine to give a licorice flavor to savory dishes. It's also an ingredient in five-spice powder. It can be found whole (star-shaped) or ground at most major grocery stores.

THAI CURRY PASTE (RED & GREEN)

A blend of aromatic herbs, fresh red chilies and fragrant herbs blended together. Used in stir-fries, curries, soups and stews. It can be found in most grocery stores, Asian supermarkets and online.

THAI RED CHILI (BIRD'S EYE CHILI)

A small spicy red or green chili—less hot than a habanero, but spicier than a jalapeño. Used in a lot of Asian cooking. Can be found in Asian supermarkets.

THAI ROASTED CHILI PASTE (NAM PRIK PRAO)

A spicy mix of puréed fruit and chili cooked down that adds a sweet, spicy and savory flavor. Can be found in some major grocery stores, Asian supermarkets and online.

(THAI) SWEET CHILI SAUCE (SPRING ROLL DIPPING SAUCE)

A chili sauce made with red chili peppers, rice wine vinegar, garlic, fish sauce and sugar. Used mainly for dips, stir-fries and noodle dishes. Can be found at some major grocery stores, Asian supermarkets, and online.

TAMARIND PASTE OR CONCENTRATE

A common ingredient in Thai cooking prepared from tamarind (a sticky and sour-tasting fruit) that adds the sour flavor to various dishes like Pad Thai. This can be found in most Asian supermarkets or online.

TOASTED SESAME OIL

An essential flavoring oil for a lot of Asian dishes. It has an intense nutty fragrance made from pressed and toasted sesame seeds. A little goes a long way, so use sparingly and add more as needed. Always look for 100 percent pure sesame oil which can be found in most major grocery stores.

Acknowledgments

Never in my dreams did I imagine myself writing a cookbook one day. Along with all the hard work and hours involved, there are so many extraordinary people to thank for helping me along this incredible ride.

To my loving mom—my inspiration, role model and biggest cheerleader. Words can't even describe how thankful I am to have you in my life. There is no one who believes in me as much as you do. Thank you for your unconditional love and support. You are the strongest, kindest and most beautiful woman I know and I feel so blessed that I can come to you and talk to you about anything. This cookbook is as much yours as it is mine and I hope I made you proud. You taught me that we can achieve anything we put our hearts into along with hard work, commitment and dedication. Even though we didn't have a lot growing up, it never stopped you from giving us all the same opportunities as everyone else—even after we lost dad. I am forever grateful that you taught us how to cook when we were younger. Those valuable skills helped tremendously when I left home to start my own family and I can only hope that I can be half the mother to my kids that you are to me. Most of all, thank you for loving them as much as I do and always being there for them . . . this is truly one of the BEST gifts you have given me.

To my husband Ty—my rock, my biggest fan, my partner in crime and my very best friend. Thank you for always encouraging and supporting me throughout this rollercoaster journey. I appreciate all those extra grocery store runs as well as the countless hours driving around to help me find the perfect props and backgrounds. Most of all, I respect the additional responsibility and hard work you took on with the house and kids, allowing me to recipe test, write and take a bazillion food photos. I am in awe that no matter what kind of crazy day it has been, you always manage to have a smile and love the three of us unconditionally. Just the adoring way you look at us takes my breath away—I couldn't have asked for a better partner in life. <3

To papa Eric, I am so grateful that you came into mom's life after dad was gone. You were willing to take on that father figure, and although at times it was hard, you never gave up. You made us feel like a family again and I wouldn't be where I am today if you didn't come along. Thank you for all your love, support and advice.

To my kids, Ethan and Evelyn, the two reasons why life was made sweeter. I never knew how much my heart could hold until becoming a mom. You both make me strive to be a better person and I can only hope I inspire you to chase your dreams.

To my brothers H & M, thank you for helping to make growing up such a fun adventure.

To my sweet in-laws, thank you all for welcoming and treating me like I was a part of the family from day one. Your love and support mean so much to me.

To the team at Page Street Publishing, especially Will, Marissa and Meg. I really appreciate the faith you had in my writing and photography from the beginning. Thank you for seeing something in me that I never would have dreamed possible.

To my dear readers, foodie friends and blogging buddies of Life Made Sweeter. Without your support, encouragement and feedback, the blog and this cookbook would not be here today. I appreciate every visit, every comment and every share; you all inspire me to continue on this journey. Thank you so much from the bottom of my heart!

About the Author

KELLY KWOK is the writer, recipe developer and photographer behind Life Made Sweeter. She started the food blog in 2013 as a creative outlet and focuses on sharing classic Asian recipes with her own modern spin, as well as easy family-friendly meals and delectable desserts.

When Kelly isn't in the kitchen creating recipes or taking photos of food for a client, she can be found spending time with her family. She is a mom of two active kids and married to her high school sweetheart.

Kelly creates recipes and videos for various brands and is a contributor for Parade Magazine Online. Her work has been featured on numerous websites such as Country Living, Better Homes and Gardens, Huffington Post, The Food Network Canada, MSN.com, Buzzfeed, Delish and more!

Index